ADVANCE PRAISE FOR *FRICTIONLESS*

We implemented Tim's Frictionless system for a win/win negotiation—it was an easy change, and it has had a massive impact at the dealership. This one little thing has helped us sell more cars, hold more gross, and make happier customers. Putting in Tim's removable objections has increased confidence in the negotiation process for both the customers and the salespeople. Tim Kintz and his new, forward thinking has been a breath of fresh air. There is not another trainer around like him! His thumb is always on the pulse.

—KELLY BALMER, SALES MANAGER, STEELTOWN FORD

I used to be intimidated negotiating with customers. Averaging only twelve cars a month, I had a lack of confidence in closing and generally in what I was doing in sales.

Once I discovered Tim Kintz, everything changed. I studied his systems and implemented his methods. With my newfound knowledge, I was suddenly able to get customers committed more quickly and was able to transition them into a negotiation more smoothly.

I gained a huge amount of confidence in myself by learning Tim's closing and negotiating techniques and putting them into practice! It wasn't long before I found myself averaging twenty-two cars per month and looking forward to creating win/win transactions with all of our customers!

Tim helped me turn this job into a career that I'm really excited about.

—ROSS BREUKER, SALES PROFESSIONAL,
CROWN AUTOMOTIVE GROUP

Without a doubt, Tim Kintz sets the standard for becoming a professional closer and negotiator. Frictionless is a must-read if you're ready for real-world strategies to help you close more deals, make more money, and become a top-producing salesperson.

—KELLY O'CONNELL, OWNER/OPERATING
PARTNER, HEARTLAND FORD; DEALER
COUNCIL CHAIRMAN, FORD OF CANADA

Tim is uniquely qualified to write this book, and I consider it a must-read for anyone building a career in automobile sales. He has run dealerships and trained thousands of salespeople and dealership leaders while speaking candidly and directly to the biggest challenges dealership personnel are facing today.

Tim's insight into today's customer and the sales process necessary to succeed is spot-on. I have known Tim for over two decades and consider him a friend and mentor who has helped me with his insight and inspiration.

—JIMMY ATKINSON, PRESIDENT AND CEO, AUL CORP.

In Frictionless, Tim Kintz shares the incredibly important concept of frictionless closing and negotiating as it relates to retail automotive sales, from his perspective as a global sales training expert whose work is based on the human emotions and logic of selling. Tim shows us how to let go of old beliefs, think differently, and embrace the current knowledge that's necessary for the rapidly changing consumer and industry.

—RANDY POINT, CHIEF OPERATING
OFFICER, MENHOLT AUTO GROUP

After working with Tim Kintz for over fifteen years, I can tell you that his hands-on training has helped transform our team into a powerhouse. Frictionless will not only give you the ability to effectively close and negotiate for maximum gross and volume, but it will help you deliver an exceptional experience that today's customers expect and deserve.

—JEREMY PARRISH, VICE PRESIDENT,
JIMMY BRITT AUTO FAMILY

We've used Tim Kintz ever since he started in business on his own. We are great fans of the daily videos and training he offers. The practical tools and approaches, along with the stories, help you to unleash your potential in automotive sales. His book is one of the best books on closing and negotiating in the car business that I've ever read.

—FRED BEANS, DEALER, FRED BEANS
FAMILY OF DEALERSHIPS

Tim's techniques on negotiating cannot be taken lightly. If you do what he tells you to, you are guaranteed to hold more gross and sell more cars. He gives you the proper verbiage to sound professional and confident during the entire sales process from start to finish.

Being able to stay on track and continue to push the deal forward, handling objections as they come, and making sure there is nothing left that can stall the negotiating stage is crucial. Tim breaks down all of these steps and makes sure we can master them.

When you absorb Tim's Frictionless system for closing and negotiating, there is no questioning if your customer is a buyer or not. You will know right away what might be holding each customer back, and you'll be able to select the perfect vehicle for them while asking all of the right questions.

—NANCY WENDELL, SALES MANAGER, SELKIRK GM

Today's consumer wants a buying experience that is easy, effective, and enjoyable. Time is too precious to be complicating a transaction with unnecessary process, leaving the most valuable and memorable part of the contact open to a dilution of trust and damaging your reputation.

Tim's book, *Frictionless*, will reengage your sales teams and focus them on the efficiencies required to be a high performer in today's market. With automotive consumers spending more time online and less time in the showroom, there has never been a better time to follow every step of Tim's techniques in his new book.

—DAVE RODDA, NATIONAL DIRECTOR OF
SALES FOR RENAULT AUSTRALIA

FRIC

TIM KINTZ

TION

CLOSING AND NEGOTIATING *WITH PURPOSE*

LESS

FRICTIONLESS

Closing and Negotiating with Purpose

ISBN   978-1-5445-0686-9   *Hardcover*

           978-1-5445-0684-5   *Paperback*

           978-1-5445-0685-2   *Ebook*

           978-1-5445-0687-6   *Audiobook*

To all the sales professionals, managers, and hardworking retail car people I've met through the years who had to find their own path working bell to bell and fighting the thirty-day cycle. This book is for you.

Also to my wife Kristi, my daughter Madden, and my son Cooper: I am so proud, and I love each of you with all my heart. Thank you for supporting me on this journey.

CONTENTS

INTRODUCTION

Selling cars can be the easiest high-paying job you'll ever have or the hardest low-paying job you'll ever have. It's your choice to make, but I will tell you that if you decide to be 100 percent committed to becoming a professional, you can have the life you deserve.

Chances are, most of you are like me—you never grew up wanting to be in car sales. I always say that getting into the car business is kind of like going to Denny's: you never plan to go there, you just end up there at one in the morning.

I got into the car business because of the earning potential—and because I needed a job. It's not that I regret the choice. I just didn't intend to make it. Car sales came at the end of my dream of becoming a big-league baseball player, which was an especially stressful time because I hadn't put much effort into academics.

Let me set the stage: I grew up in a small town outside of St. Louis, Missouri, in a middle-class family with the hardest working parents I've ever seen—and I dreamed of and believed I was going to be a big-league baseball player. I was lucky enough to get a baseball scholarship to a school in Arizona, so I started chasing that dream. Needless to say, academics weren't high on my priority list.

I did accomplish something that very few have or will: I spent four years in college, stayed eligible to play baseball all four years, and still didn't have enough credits to get a two-year degree.

I don't say that because it's something that I'm proud of—I say that because, regardless of your education level or choices you made in the past, I believe anyone with drive, desire, and discipline can make more money than they ever imagined if they make the right choices.

On one side of my life I saw my buddies playing ball for $15,000 to $65,000 a year, and on the other side there were the salespeople that I detailed cars for at the Honda/Acura store making $100,000 to 200,000. I made the choice to give selling cars a shot and then, like most of us, I was thrown to the wolves to figure the rest out by myself.

Now, with what feels like a lifetime of experience in just

about every role in the store and nearly two decades as a trainer, I see that story repeated more often than not, especially on the sales floor.

The story we're all told when we get hired is true. I don't know of any other career where you can make the money we make with the limited education that a lot of us have. The great thing about selling cars is that you don't have to be an elite athlete or have a college degree to make six figures.

The potential upside is amazing. If you're good, if you bust your ass, if you develop the needed skills, if you have the intestinal fortitude to survive, if you care about customers...Then yes, you will make great money and have a fantastic career.

As I said in the beginning, selling cars can be the easiest high-paying job you'll ever have or the hardest low-paying job you'll ever have. *You* are the deciding factor, and the way you approach closing and negotiating is a critical key to your success—or failure.

THE PROMISE VERSUS REALITY

Some people say that great salespeople are born. Some people believe they're made. I guess the actual answer is that it's both. At some point, great salespeople were all born—but even for people who seem like naturals, somewhere along the line, something or someone influenced them. Maybe they were in the military and that's where they learned to be disciplined. Maybe they learned to communicate and that's how they got so good with customers. Maybe they were an athlete like me—as the top pitcher, I knew that the guys behind me were working as hard as they could to take my spot. I had to work just as hard as them, if not harder, to keep my spot. That taught me so much about competition, coachability, and work ethic, and all of those skills served me well in sales.

Unfortunately, none of that shows up on the job description or in the onboarding or initial training.

Typically, the help wanted ad is all about the unlimited earning potential and how the dealership has more leads than they know what to do with. How many ads have you seen like this:

Business is booming! Have traffic, need people. Excellent pay. Control your future! Be in business for yourself—full inventory at your fingertips. We train and support!

And how long did it take for those promises to fall apart?

You pass the drug screen, have a decent driving record, and John in HR tells you that you're good to go. Then you show up Monday with a spark in your eye, spring in your step, and smile on your face—but John's nowhere to be found. Jill, one of the managers, doesn't even know who you are. She welcomes you aboard anyway and sends you off to the showroom floor to get to know the team. Two hours later, you go looking for Jill, who's forgotten you're even there. She introduces you to Steve—the loyal, under-achieving six-car guy—and asks him to get you up to speed.

That guy shows you the new cars, the used cars, the key board with all the keys, and sets you up in the CRM. He takes you upstairs to watch the OEM product training videos and leaves, where you sit for hours on end to get certified and hope you don't fall asleep.

Eventually, you emerge from the shadows and they part-ner you back up with six-car Steve. Someone will walk onto the lot and they tell you to take that "up" and do the best you can—just as long as you don't let them go without talking to a manager first.

Sure, we all make some sales and can get pretty good grosses on them. Especially early on, when enthusiasm takes over. We assume everyone's a buyer. We go on demos because *we* want to drive the car more than the customer does, and we don't get into price conversations. We haven't had time to build bad habits, customers like us, and we make it through just fine.

Then the Ninety-Day Wonder kicks in: ninety days later, you wonder why you can't sell cars.

BECOMING THE EXPERT IN THE PEOPLE BUSINESS

Even though we all know that a large part of success comes from repeatable processes, in most stores there are none for us to follow. We get minimal training, few resources, and whatever support we're lucky enough to latch on to. Settling in under these conditions was hard enough when I got started—new folks today are selling to customers who often know more than we do about the product and process, and we have decades of a less-than-honest reputation to overcome. Relevant, belly-to-belly sales training has never been more important, and it's just as hard to get as ever.

You'll hear war stories about how we used to be able to make so much more on a car. That was then, and this is now. Today, manufacturers have compressed the profit margin so far that we have to get creative to make a reasonable profit. Customers aren't just dividing a car price by sixty and expecting that to be their payment—they have payment calculators and trade values and price comparisons from all competitors, including traditional and newer nontraditional competitors. We can't skate by with surface skills anymore. It's an uphill battle.

The whole dynamic is a shame, really. I don't want to

know more about what's wrong with me than my doctor knows. The problem is, customers don't think of us as the experts anymore. They've dealt with too many amateurs to believe otherwise.

Listen, I realize that all businesses change and evolve. Selling cars isn't the same today as it was ten, fifteen, or even twenty years ago. I get it—in fact, a lot of what I'll teach you in this book has to do with the way the car business is evolving and how we need to grow with it. But the bottom line is that we're still in the people business.

If you want to guarantee your current and future success in sales, you need to be the expert. You need to know how to deliver an exceptional customer experience every time. That starts by setting up and executing a successful win-win negotiation, and ultimately selling the car the right way the first time so you can manage the customer's trade cycle.

If we want to become the expert, rediscover those first months' excitement, and enjoy a sustainable career in car sales, we clearly have some work to do. And it's not fun. Practice is boring. I can't even compare it to sports, because hitting golf balls and shooting free throws is fun. At least then you can see the results and get some instant gratification. Practicing selling scripts doesn't come with any result or reward until it's been mastered.

As Hall of Fame quarterback Roger Staubach famously said, "Any spectacular achievement was preceded by a bunch of unspectacular practice."

If we want to make this industry work for us, we have to get to work on ourselves, even when it feels like unspectacular practice.

PERFECT PRACTICE MAKES PERFECT

Everybody wants to be great at closing and negotiating, but all too often we just want to pick up a book full of tips and skim it until we find a magic pill. We don't want to do the work, or maybe we don't know what work we need to do. Everyone wants to be great, but only the truly great are willing to pay the price for that greatness.

This book doesn't have a magic pill, but it does have the knowledge and skills you need to be more effective at closing sales and negotiating deals.

That limitless earning potential we're all promised is payment for the work you do *between* customers, not on them. It's gathering knowledge, yes, but knowledge alone is dangerous in the car business. It makes you think you can do things when you can't.

Knowledge doesn't make sales. What I tell every class

I've trained is that when you think, you stink—it needs to become your instinct.

> Knowledge + Skills + Confidence = Enthusiasm—and enthusiasm sells!
>
> Remember: sales are made when you transfer your enthusiasm to the customer.

I'm going to give you knowledge in this book that you might not have yet. We'll talk about what today's customers want and need, and how you can become the expert.

I'm also going to give you the skills you need to close well and to treat negotiating as the lost art that it is.

But the only way you're going to gain confidence is to practice.

Vince Lombardi said, "Amateurs practice 'til they get it right, pros practice 'til they can't get it wrong." That's what we're going for. We need our knowledge and skills to be so ingrained that they become our reflexes.

When a customer says, "We're just going to think about it," that's a ninety-mile-an-hour fastball coming at your bat. You don't have time to think about whether you should swing or not. You have to just know. Only real confidence shows up to respond in those cases.

When you're confident, you're enthusiastic, and enthusiasm sells cars.

If you're ready for perfect practice—for a lot of work and a brand-new perspective—keep reading. I'll set you up with what you need to know to understand closing and negotiating, from concept to best practices. I'll teach you how to create a win/win relationship with your customers and show you how it will improve your sales cycle. The work you do here will make your job that much easier in the long run.

Whether you're currently at the top of the sales board, at the bottom of the sales board, new to the business, a long-term vet, or somewhere in between—whether you're at a one-price store, something more progressive, or on an old-school sales floor—the world has changed too much to carry on without having the sharpest closing and negotiating skills. Time's wasting, and time is money—so let's get started.

PART I

UNDERSTANDING FRICTION

CHAPTER 1

THE PAST, PRESENT, AND FUTURE OF CLOSING AND NEGOTIATING

THE GHOST OF CAR SALES PAST

Let's clear this up right away: the good old days weren't all that good. They're just old. The way car sales happened in the early years gave us a bad reputation, and not without cause. For a little while, "used car salesman" ranked just above (sometimes below) politicians and lawyers. Folks would rather be sued or maybe even get a root canal before they chose to buy a car. (At least with the root canal they might get free drugs!) And we in the industry haven't been too excited about the process either.

Manufacturers have compressed our margins down to nothing. The economic upswing brought people in the doors, but since they're armed with more information and we're stuck with less preparation, we all got caught up in volume mindset rather than thinking about what was best for everyone.

DON'T LET THE FEAR OF LOSING THE SALE KEEP YOU FROM HAVING FUN

Computer programs with professional-looking worksheets started spitting numbers out to us, and without any training to tell us otherwise, we started to think that's all there was to wrapping up a deal. Now, one-price stores and nontraditional options have started popping up, and the projections all point to Amazon-style online click-and-buy being the next big wave.

Somewhere along the line, closing has been forgotten and negotiating has become a dirty word.

I think we've just forgotten where we truly came from—not from sleazy salesmen and underhanded tricks, but the true art of the negotiation that humans have been practicing since the dawn of time. The kind that lets everyone walk away feeling like they've won. The kind that comes from inspiration to make a deal that works rather than desperation to not lose another deal.

In order to get back to the lost art of closing and negotiating, first we have to unwind the last few decades of car sales. Where did we come from as an industry, and where are we going next?

THE EVOLUTION OF THE FOUR-SQUARE

Back when my parents were buying their first cars, they would go to the dealership when a new car was launching, then order the model, color, and accessories they wanted. The salesperson would give them a little card that showed what they were going to get, and more often than not, they would pay cash on the spot. If they decided to finance, then they would get a purchase order first, and they'd take it to their bank or credit union to get a loan for it on their own. When the car came in, the dealer would call them, they'd pick it up, and that would be that. No dealer financing, no aftermarket product—just a quick and easy delivery of their brand-new car.

Up until the '70s or '80s, very little about this process changed.

Eventually, someone realized that we could make another couple hundred dollars from each sale if we could provide more than the car itself. We could finance cars right there at the dealership instead of sending them off to banks. We could sell products like extended service contracts and insurance for the life of the loan. The banks let dealerships start financing and printing contracts right there in the finance department, and suddenly car sales became a one-stop-shop.

With more than just price, trade, and difference on the table, negotiating on price alone wasn't effective at maximizing gross anymore. After all, more customers were making finance payments, so the total price didn't matter as much. The two main things that we needed to focus on now were payment and down payment.

That's how the four-square—price, trade, payment, and down payment—was born.

For over thirty years, this worksheet was the basis of all negotiations, and many dealerships still use it today. Whatever we had to give and take in a deal went into one of those four boxes, and we worked it out from there. Even today's more complex systems usually have their basis in those four factors. Everything from a Sharpie on a blank sheet of paper to a cool color printout and everything in between is more or less a four-square.

This was the mindset behind negotiation for decades: where can we find room and hold gross by using and manipulating payments and down payments?

Then the 2000s hit, and everything changed.

THE GREAT RECESSION

Around 2008, the economy took the biggest hit it had seen in a generation, and our industry took the brunt of it. We were worried every time FedEx pulled onto the lot, because they could be carrying a letter from the manufacturer saying they had pulled the franchise.

We went in every morning not sure if we'd have a job by the end of the day. So, the last thing we were about to do was to work the customer too hard and show them options like 20 percent down with short-term financing. Even if it was the best way to get the car, we couldn't survive without every deal we could get, and they couldn't survive with that kind of expense. The whole country was in desperation mode, and we did whatever we had to do just to sell the car.

Negotiating was the first thing that went out the door.

We lost a lot of good people in the car business in that era. They got tired of the uncertainty and took their hard-earned skills to more stable industries. Those vacancies were usually filled with brand-new people who had never been taught how to close and negotiate—for many of the younger generation, they had never even been exposed to a real negotiation process.

If you came in during or after the recession, chances are you were shown "negotiation" that looked like giving customers options that printed out of a computer, hoping they'd pick one, then turning them over to F&I, where they secured the deal and sold aftermarket products.

Too many of us became offer presenters rather than negotiators. And thanks to the way the internet exploded right around the recession, this made win/win deals tougher to create.

NEGOTIATING IN THE INFORMATION AGE

When a brand-new house goes up for sale, the builder doesn't tell you, "Well, our cost on it was $186,000, so we're going to start there and negotiate up." There's plenty of negotiation in a home purchase, but no one in that industry is racing to the bottom. They're not shrugging their shoulders and thinking, *Well, even if we took a little loss, at least we got that house sold.*

Even if you want to think of car sales more like retail, the grocery store doesn't tell you what they paid for that can of soup. We make our choices based on other things, like perceived value and how nice it will be to enjoy that soup on a rainy day.

For a long time, the same was true for car sales. The customers didn't know what our profit margin was or how the numbers really worked out—they just knew they wanted the car and they needed it to fit into their budget.

Then came the internet, and the real game changer: the smartphone. Now, not only can consumers do incredible amounts of research on their computers at home before they ever step onto the lot, but they can run searches right there on the lot to get all the information that they need. Companies like TrueCar will tell them what a fair price on the car is, based on what everyone else has paid; payment calculators will do the budget work for them (and us); and every dealer's searchable inventory will help them shop around in a matter of minutes.

It's not a bad thing for customers to be more informed, unless we don't adapt our sales process to match.

Running away from technology isn't going to be the answer, but neither is leaning on it too heavily. Sometimes we like to think that having a pretty worksheet with lots of options on it is a negotiation, but it's only part of it. If you can't negotiate based on those options, then the customer will pick the lowest down payment with the lowest payment and that's that. We're still just presenting offers, usually while running back and forth as middlemen between the customer and the manager.

Once you get good at negotiating, you could literally put numbers down on a napkin and make the customer feel like they've won. Until then, it doesn't matter what tools you use—you won't be able to make that win/win deal happen.

Technology doesn't take buyers from us and technology doesn't sell cars. People sell cars. And sometimes, people who have the skills will use technology to sell those cars. But at the end of the day, we're in the people business. We need to be careful to remember that, or these fears about vending machines, kiosks, and Amazon taking over the car business might just come true.

Hey, I know it's tempting to jump right into the later chapters where all the meat is—but there's a reason we're taking it slow. The more you know why you're doing something, the better you can execute the how. Stick with me for now, and if you really want some tools and immediate resources, head over to frictionlessnegotiating.com.

1 . 2

COMPETING IN THE CURRENT MARKET

In the past, any given dealership was just in competition with the dealer down the street. If someone could easily drive to another store from yours, that was who you were up against. The skills in your store had to be better than the skills in theirs, and a person might plan on driving around to compare the two.

Now, we're competing against every dealership in the country.

Today's consumers are a click away from not only exploring but actually buying from anyone they want to with just an internet browser and a smartphone. That doesn't even include the nontraditional companies that are entering our marketplace. Take Carvana, for example. Their advertised value is that there is no salesperson—for *you* to deal with. Just a rotating tower of cars that will drop your choice to you like a sandwich out of a vending machine. If that's not direct-to-consumer enough, Amazon is rumored to be working on getting their foot in the door too.

Before, when our competition was just the guy down the street, he was going to be an offer presenter too. He was going to take five hours to sell someone a car too. He was going to miss out on building value and forget to follow up too. Everyone was struggling in the same ways, so we didn't have to level up. We didn't have to work to stand out.

Now, we can't pinpoint our competition to a specific place—it's literally the whole world. I can get on my smartphone and buy a car from Sewell Ford in Odessa while I'm driving through Austin and have it sitting in my driveway in Dallas when I get home. So if it's not *who* or *where* our competition is, let's take a few moments to unpack *what* exactly we're competing against in today's market.

IT'S ABOUT MORE THAN PRICE

One clue about the way people think of us shows up in post-sale numbers: it's estimated that in 2018 consumers spent somewhere around $394 billion on vehicle mainte-nance and care, and dealerships only captured about $65 billion of that.[1] That means our dealerships potentially lost $329 billion—and probably a customer in the process.

When you understand the industry, this makes no sense. The labor rate at a third-party shop is likely going to be as high or higher than what the average dealership charges, so why are people taking their cars to Jiffy Lube for an oil change instead of the dealership? Price seems like an obvious answer, but it's only one factor. It just *seems* cheaper and more convenient because people associate us with cost and a hassle. The perception and experience are what matters, not the actual numbers.

We can understand this in other areas of life. For example, when you shop at Amazon, you're not getting the best deal every time, and it doesn't matter. It's the conve-nience that creates value. When it comes to cars, people are just as willing to pay more money for the perception of convenience—and it's up to us to make their experience with us the better option.

In reality, few dealerships have earned the trust and con-

---

1   Renee Bailey, "Auto Franchise Industry Report 2018," Franchise Direct, December 17, 2018, https://www.franchisedirect.com/information/auto-franchise-industry-report-2018; National Automobile Dealers Association, "NADA Data 2018 Annual Financial Profile of America's Franchised New-Car Dealerships," https://www.nada.org/WorkArea/DownloadAsset. aspx?id=21474857318. These sales are based on service labor and parts sales for customer mechanical, warranty, and sublet.

fidence of their customers, from the difficult sales process to the lack of follow-through afterward.

Imagine a relationship where you call your customers to help them schedule their next oil change, and they call you when they're ready to get another car:

> "Hey, Bill, this is what we're looking at getting. What are your thoughts?"

Think about how negotiating to get them into a forty-eight to sixty-month term would show them that you're looking out for them, and when they do give you that call about a new car, they're in a good equity position to trade up. And yes, you've made money on the deal, but you don't feel bad about it because it's part of your job. Imagine your customers really trusting you and valuing your role because you've been there when they've needed you, so they negotiate from a place of openness rather than distrust.

Even though these are all attainable things, more often than not, we create a terrible experience on the lot, get them into something they *think* they want but that will hurt them in the long run—and then we don't ever speak to them again.

Customers aren't just shopping for the lowest price.

Buying a car isn't just transactional—it's an emotional experience. They do their research before they go out because they want something that will feel good to own and they don't want to get screwed trying to buy it. We're competing against anyone who will respect their time, earn their trust, and deliver an exceptional experience around an emotional purchase. If we can do a good job, it changes their expectations forever and can create a customer for life.

DISRUPTED PATTERNS

I can walk onto just about any lot in the country and expect the same exact experience. Someone will greet me, and then soon after ask me, "How much are you looking to spend?" Then they'll show me a bunch of inventory, then bring me inside whether or not I'm showing any sort of commitment, and set me down with a multi-payment worksheet. I might pick the lowest numbers on the sheet that won't make them any money at all. They won't care— four or five hours in, they just want to get me out of there with some kind of sale.

If you want to stand out from the competition, it's time to disrupt that pattern.

Make it all about the customer. Find out about them and their car first—not just for trade value, but what they like and don't like about it, what's important for their next car, and why they're out there looking in the first place. Avoid the data-dump presentations, because they've already done the research and know why they want it.

If a salesperson were to meet me at a Ford Raptor and start talking about horsepower and suspension and off-roading, I would walk away. I just like those trucks because they look badass, are comfortable, and have cool interior features. Off-roading does me no good at all when it's going to spend twenty days a month at an airport parking lot. Unless they disrupt the pattern that every other salesperson follows—unless they make it about me—they're not going to earn my business.

If they show up asking me about what I like about my current truck, they'll learn that I love my twenty-two-inch wheels, the lift, and the black on black. They'll learn what I'm looking for and help me find that in the best Raptor for me. More importantly, this will show me that they're different from every other salesperson I've encountered. They're disrupting the pattern, and I'm going to be more open to what they have to say because of it.

That's why we're going to talk about the buyer's perspective before we get into a better sales process. When we focus on what the customer cares about—not what we care about—we can better figure out the best way to get them into a new vehicle. We can find something that meets their needs, wants, and budget. Then, when we sit down to negotiate, we'll know the benefits that will be helpful and appealing for them, the options that they'll want, and the variables that will pull out their top number and start the negotiation from a position of strength versus a position of weakness. All along the way, they'll be more relaxed and open to what we have to say, because it's a different experience than they've ever had before.

ZERO-SUM GAME

The worst thing you can hear in a dealership is a salesperson on the phone saying, "Oh...you did...thanks."

On the other end of the line, the customer is saying, "We got the car from someone else—but you were the *nicest* salesperson we've ever talked to, and *next time* we're definitely going to buy from you."

They'll tell you that it wasn't about you. They'll probably blame their spouse for liking another car better. But one thing's for sure: they're absolutely *not* going to buy from you next time. If you're too scared to close or negotiate, you're not going to be in business long.

The thing is, people want to negotiate. If there's just one price to work with and no other variables to give and take, they're going to walk away feeling like they left money on the table. Even if it was a great deal, they want to know they worked for it a little bit and earned a better deal. It's the drive to haggle that we've had as long as humans have been trading with each other.

The best salespeople know this, and they value their part in that process. They take it personally if they have to sell a car without making any money, because that means the customer didn't see value in them either. We might as well give them our ATM cards and pin numbers and let them withdraw money right from our checking accounts.

YOU EITHER CLOSE *OR LOSE–* A CLOSER *OR A LOSER*

As low as our margins for profit are these days, there's hardly any room for error. If you're afraid to go out there and negotiate with your customer and they leave to go to another dealership who will, they won't be back. The "I don't want them to think I'm trying to sell them" attitude isn't going to do you any favors. Another salesperson won't worry about being pushy, and when they make the sale, they won't send you a referral fee from their commission just because you were nice.

The thing is, we don't have to be pushy to be effective at closing and negotiating. The difference between persistence and pressure is technique. It's not always what you say but how you say it—if you haven't internalized the skills through practice, you might come across as pushy. But the only way to get over that hump and get better is to do it.

This is a zero-sum game. You'll sell to them or someone else will—and the more we give customers a bad experience at dealerships, the more automated processes are going to win.

> If we want to move into a frictionless future, it helps to know where we've been. Even if you're brand-new to the business, I bet you can think of changes in the market just since you started, or maybe since you first bought a car. Take a minute to think about how things have changed. Maybe write them down. The business is going to keep changing from here on in—the trick is going to be keeping people at the center of it all.

CALMING THE FEAR OF THE FUTURE

How worried are we, really, that kiosks are going to sell cars one day? How much is click-and-buy really going to take from us? I can't say for sure, but I can tell you that you're missing the point if you try to use those nontraditional disruptors, like Carvana, as examples and excuses to not even try to negotiate. It's not the negotiation process that customers want to avoid—they hate dealing with the *amateur* salesperson and their long sales process.

Right now, the overwhelming majority of car sales still happen belly-to-belly, face-to-face, person-to-person. The only way the computers win in the future is if we give up on good skills right here in the present.

If you want to guarantee a future success in sales, getting your closing and negotiating skills down is your very first step. Give customers an exceptional experience that they can enjoy, that makes them feel like they've won and makes them want to come back for more. Build a relationship on trust—one where you both value your role because of the way you serve the customer.

Stop worrying about what the future might hold for your career or your industry and start focusing on how you can make every deal as good as it can possibly be right now. That's what will carry us into the future.

Sustainable car sales isn't just about grabbing every customer that comes through, but about maximizing those opportunities for both parties. It's a creative effort, not a reactive one. If we win and they lose, we might make a lot of money right then, but they'll hate our guts and never come back for more. If they steal the car and we don't make any money, a lose/win deal, they might still be frustrated with the experience if they had to grind it out, and we'll be left with a loss. A win/win outcome— where we make money and they are happy with the whole experience—is not only possible, but it should be our ultimate goal.

And listen, I'll never ask you to walk away from a deal just because it's not win/win. We don't lose sales just because we think we have to hit a certain number, but losing money should be a last resort—the customer has to earn that deal. I often say that we can boil a negotiation down to four simple rules: hold gross, hold gross, hold gross, and if you can't hold gross, sell the car. Unfortunately, too many of us jump right to rule number four and just *sell the car*.

Surprisingly, that's exactly what the customer expects to see from us in the first place.

WHAT CUSTOMERS WANT

Let's go back to home purchases for just a minute. Think about why you might put an offer in on a house. If your realtor is good, it's probably because you can visualize your family living there. You walk into one room and decide that it will be your daughter's, and she asks if she can paint it purple and hang her pictures on the walls. Then the kids run into another room and ask if it can be the game room. You see where your home office will go, or where the TV fits in the living room. Before you ever put an offer in, you've taken mental ownership of the house. When you walk out the door, you're already mentally moving your furniture in before the negotiation has even started.

Now, even though you're the one to make an offer, who started the negotiation? You didn't get to weigh your budget against the cost to build the house—they set the price. Their asking price started the negotiation, and by showing up to look at it, you showed your top-end numbers. Now the haggling happens over a lower price, but also closing costs, new paint, and carpet allowances.

Do you really care about the paint or the carpet allowance? Probably not. You just want to get a good deal on the house you already want to own. When they come back and say they'll do *this* and *this* but not *that*, you're happy. You've already decided what's going on the walls and in the floor plan—in your mind, that house is yours. The rest is just about the best way to make it happen. This is the kind of negotiation that we enjoy—it makes us feel good about the experience and even better about the purchase itself.

So why does it *feel* like everyone hates to negotiate?

If we look at a car deal the same way we look at real estate, it becomes clear that we're doing things backwards. We try to get people to financially purchase the car before they've taken mental ownership.

Think about it. What's one of the first things almost every salesperson will say when you walk onto a lot?

Hey, folks. Just so I can point you in the right direction—how much are you looking to spend a month? How much down do you have? What do you owe on your trade?

You've got no emotional attachment at that point. You don't see how you can put your kids' gear in the back, or how you could have used new back-up camera technology the other day, or how hitch assist would help with launching your boat.

The conversation started the negotiation, and it took away any excitement the customer had when they walked onto the lot. Not to mention when the customer gives us their numbers, they lowball us. The end result is a complete lack of credibility and a battle in the negotiation.

When they tell us $300 a month with zero down is all they can do and later you hit them with $6,700 down and $784.14 per month, it becomes a grind. Even if we make the deal, it'll result in low to no gross and a negative customer perception.

Every bit of this can be avoided if we approach our customer interactions differently.

Think about what it looks like to build a car online—our supposed enemy. You decide you want a truck, and you're going to spec it out before you go out to the dealership. Does the website start by asking you what you want to pay per month, how much down you have, or what you owe on your trade?

No, it has you build out the features first.

You're picking the trim and interior colors, the panoramic sunroof and the USB ports in the back. Every feature that you click on is connected to some personal need in your mind, and you get more and more excited as the details come together. By the end, you have a $50,000 car that you never would have volunteered in the beginning. And it doesn't matter, because you're emotionally invested.

CLOSE ON EMOTION, NEGOTIATE ON LOGIC

Closing and negotiating are two sides of the same coin—closing relies on emotion and seeing the value that exists outside of numbers, and negotiation relies on logic. The art of this process is in leveraging emotion to justify the logic. It's painting the vehicle into the customer's life, solving problems, getting the customer licking the paint off the car, and then fitting it into their budget.

Instead of starting with budget and bouncing numbers back and forth between your customer and manager, what might it look like to have a conversation like this:

Customer: I don't think we can afford $670.

*I understand $670 is more than your current payment of $535.
If I could show you how you could save over $100 per month
on this new car, would you drive it home?*

Customer: Of course I would.

*Well, earlier you said you drive about seventy-five miles a day
and your current car gets fifteen miles per gallon. This new one
gets twenty-five. So that means you're using five gallons per
day on your current car and only three gallons on this new one.
That's a savings of about sixty gallons per month. With gas at
three bucks a gallon, that's $180 saved in real cash every month.*

*Plus you said you've spent about $1,000 in repairs this year,
so that's another $80 per month.*

*So I understand that you're only paying $535 to the bank, but
your total cost of ownership is $795 per month. Your new pay-
ment is only $670, so that's $125 in real money you'll be saving
every month with this new car.*

Do you want your payment in thirty or forty-five days?

They won't just lie down and pay top dollar every time,
but it's our job to help them justify it and help them make
sense of it.

Stop asking for numbers and promising to make them

work. Stop acting out of amateurish desperation. Stop trying to be the one-stop-shop and start leveraging their emotions and logic to help them get what they really want and deserve.

RECOGNIZE, INTERNALIZE, CUSTOMIZE

As we move into the sales process, first from the buyer's perspective and then from ours as salespeople, you're going to recognize skills that will make win/win deals for both you and your customers. This isn't a book that you can just read and then the skills will suddenly come to you in a dream one night and change your life. It takes practice. I think of that work happening on three levels: recognize, internalize, customize.

Listen to two people sing the United States national anthem. Do they sound the same? Not at all. We recognize it by the lyrics, but reading the words by themselves would sound kind of ridiculous. Everyone puts their own spin on how it sounds, and that's how we appreciate the meaning of the song.

It's the same for the skills we need to develop in sales. Once you recognize the things that work—the words, techniques, and focus you need to have—and you decide to internalize them, the first stage of practice begins. Like learning the lyrics to a song, you read them over and over again, listen to them, internalize and practice them backward, forward, and sideways. Only once you know them inside and out can you start to customize them.

AMATEURS PRACTICE UNTIL THEY GET IT RIGHT

PROFESSIONALS
PRACTICE
UNTIL THEY
CAN'T
GET IT WRONG

Whenever I teach scripts, tips, and techniques, I expect people to internalize and then customize them. You should recognize a great close that would help you out, or a new way to engage in a negotiation, then read it over and over, word for word, until you know it well. Then, once you've internalized it so that it becomes second nature, you can customize it—make it more like you, the way Nelly and Alan Jackson could each sing the same song and make it sound completely different.

Together, we're going to work on disrupting patterns, focusing on the customer, building the value higher than the price, and leveraging the emotions of closing and the logic of negotiation. There are a lot of skills to learn, and it will take practice to get them right.

Recognize, internalize, customize, and you can turn your uncertain sales job into a sustainable career.

> The real fear we all have for the future is that customers will choose someone or something else over us. Take a few minutes to think about the problems kiosks solve—faster process, a sense of expertise, the customer getting the experience they want—and how your sales process does or doesn't meet those needs. Now don't panic. We'll cover a better sales process in the book, but first, let's get to know the customer a little better.

CHAPTER 2

THE BUYER'S JOURNEY

BEFORE THE LOT

Five or six years ago, my wife Kristi decided that she wanted to get a Jeep Grand Cherokee. For her, pre-lot research was simple: she saw one and decided she liked it. Some people need to build it out online to connect with each of the specs; others are emotionally attached right away. That's how my wife felt about potentially getting a new Jeep. She didn't need to know much about it to know that she wanted one.

So together, we drove to a local car lot, ready to look at her options. We told them what we were looking for— we knew the Grand Cherokee was it, but we were open on the trim level. We probably wanted something pretty loaded but wanted to see the differences between them in person.

The next thing you know, we're wandering the lot with a

salesperson. Now instead of knowing the one model we wanted, we have sixty versions of it to choose from, each with different prices and colors and options...I could see Kristi getting more and more overwhelmed.

When we finally got to one that looked like it was pretty nice and close to what she wanted, the salesperson said, "Do you want to drive it?"

After all that effort to get to the lot for a specific car she knew she wanted, and after all that time going around the lot to find the exact right one, *does she want to drive it?* Well...no. She actually said no, and we left without a Grand Cherokee. In fact, she's still driving the vehicle we took to the lot that day.

The salesperson lost a sale that day, not only for himself but for his dealership and anyone around him. A lot of things went wrong—but the number one problem was that he wasn't thinking about Kristi's wants, needs, and mindset. Things that were happening for her before she ever stepped foot on the lot.

"I THINK IT'S TIME TO GET A NEW CAR."

At some point before you ever see that customer step onto the lot, they decided it was time to get a new car. Whether it's one spouse saying it to the other, a new addition joining the family, a new job that calls for an upgrade, or a pain point that requires something newer or safer—something sparked that visit to the lot.

It might be a clear lightbulb moment or a slow burn over time. It might be an immediate need or a more easygoing curiosity. It might take them six months of research or six hours of thought. Some people are measured, and others are spontaneous.

The timeline before they make it to the lot will vary, and it doesn't really matter—the important thing to remember is that everyone has a compelling reason to be there. Even if it's not a reason that compels you, their reason for getting out and stepping onto your lot is compelling to them.

For Kristi, that Jeep was more of a pleasure point than a pain point. It would have been nice to have a new car that looked better than the one she had, though the one she had was fine. If the salesperson had taken the time to understand that about her, he would have known just how easy it would be to chase her away, and how easy it would be to help her get the new Jeep she wanted. She had a compelling reason to go out that day with every intention of buying, but the salesperson needed to compel her to stay. Instead, he chased her off with complicated details.

Customers who show up with broken down cars or a new

baby on the way—pain point buyers—need that car. Just don't screw it up and they'll probably make the purchase.

For anyone who doesn't absolutely need that vehicle, it's easy to become a sales-prevention person. If you don't connect with them, if they don't trust you, if they're not engaged, then you're dead in the water. They'll only put up with so much of our archaic process before they decide the effort isn't worth it.

> It's harder to talk a pain point buyer out of the sale, but that's not everyone's story. Be careful that you don't become a sales-prevention person for the pleasure point buyer, and always get the buyer's background story to know which is which.

"I WANT TO GO CHECK THAT OUT."

So many dealers are still following processes that were set in place ten, twenty, thirty years ago, even though today's buyers are not the same at all. While we're taught to memorize specs and rattle them off during the presentation and demonstration, most of our buyers show up with that information already.

It happens on different levels for everyone. Some people are completely emotional in their research, like my wife. She'll talk to friends who drive the vehicle that interests her to see if they like it. She'll make her choice based on what looks good to her, and that's all it takes.

Other people do their research from a completely logical standpoint. They think about their commute and decide an electric or hybrid version might be a good fit, so they learn all there is to know about hybrid cars. They find out where they can charge it and how far it will take them. Some people do full builds on the internet and send out inquiries directly to dealerships to see what they have that matches.

Not only are the details top of mind whenever they make it to the lot, but they've been thinking about the car long enough that it's emotional as well—even for the most logical researcher.

If I get curious about a Tahoe and start to build it out on GM's website, that damn Tahoe is going to follow me around the internet no matter where I go. All my sidebar ads and banner ads on Facebook and Amazon and everywhere else will hold that data cookie and remind me that I had been looking at a Tahoe. Now my subconscious is in on it and my compelling reason is now that much more insistent.

> Buyers know more than we do these days. They don't need us to overwhelm them with more information than they already have—they need us to validate their emotional instincts and help them seal the deal.

"ARE WE SURE IT'S THE RIGHT TIME?"

Even though Kristi did in fact want to drive that car, the yes or no question triggered a reflexive "no." Sometimes the customer has already driven it, or they want to feel good about the price first, or they're just scared to commit. There are a lot of logical reasons they might decide not to test-drive, but there's something else happening under the surface.

The thing is, we didn't drive all the way out there to *not* test-drive a Jeep Grand Cherokee. Nobody takes their family out car shopping just for the heck of it. I've never asked my wife what she wanted to do on a Saturday and she said, "Let's go to a car dealership—that'll be a fun way to spend our weekend." But if we give them an out, they're going to take it. Why? Because customers show up both excited and nervous.

It's the buyer's dilemma—the customer's burden. They come to the dealership with every intention to spend the money, but they're nervous about spending the money. It's like having buyer's remorse in advance.

Because that salesperson didn't consider anything about my wife's needs, wants, or mindset before she ever walked onto the lot, he worked up all the wrong emotions leading up to the demo, which would have been the highest emotional point of the sale. By showing her too many choices, he shut down all of the excitement and curiosity and amplified all of the stress and anxiety; it's no surprise that fight-or-flight instinct kicked in as soon as he opened up that yes or no window of escape.

> Buyers are there because they want to buy. Validate their excitement and show them how perfect that vehicle is for them. Convince them that they made the right choice to show up to your lot that day.

John Maxwell says that people don't care how much you know until they know how much you care. I don't think he's ever sold cars, but I would bet that he could have done a better job of it that day than the salesperson who met me and Kristi on the lot.

Every buyer is going to be compelled by something different. Every buyer will have their own level of research and inspiration. Every buyer will have their doubts about whether they're making the right decision, and a whole lot of concerns about how difficult the process is going to be.

Assume that they are, in fact, buyers; learn where they are and how they're showing up that day; and meet them where they are so you can take them to the car of their dreams.

Sometimes, the best way to understand your customer is to remember the last time you were a customer yourself. Did you enjoy anything about the process? Were you surprised at all, or did they deliver exactly what you expected? Did you wind up becoming a buyer? The next time you're on the lot with an up, put yourself in their shoes. How would you want to be treated? That's what the next section's all about.

THE BUYER'S QUADRANT

Every person who walks onto the lot is different, and that's exactly why we have to treat them all the same. By that, I mean we can't prequalify who can handle shortcuts in the sales process and who needs special handling.

We can't know by looking at someone whether they've done a lot of research for their pain point or are there spontaneously for a pleasure point. Even if we could, it wouldn't get us out of any of our selling responsibilities. The emotional, spontaneous person still needs some logic to ground their decision, and the logical researcher still needs a world-class experience to raise the emotional value to match the cost when they built the car out online.

The only assumptions that we can make are:

1. Everyone who shows up on the lot has some intention to buy.
2. Every buyer has a similar pathway toward trust that we have to guide them through.

I call this process the Buyer's Quadrant, and it holds true for everyone, from the lifetime repeat customer to the customer you've never met before in your life. Each emotional step is revisited every time—sometimes a few times within a deal.

BUYERS QUADRANT
(SALES QUADRANT)

1

GUARDED
(REASSURE THE
CUSTOMER)

2

**OPEN-
MINDED**
(HIGH-IMPACT
PRESENTATION)

3

CONFIDENT
(TRANSITION THE
CUSTOMER)

4

TRUST
(WIN/WIN
TRANSACTION)

QUADRANT 1: GUARDED

The buyer's dilemma is on full display when they first step onto the lot. All of their excitement and all of their nerves are front and center. With all of those emotions at play, they're going to be guarded. Every experience they've had with dealerships or heard before tells them to distrust us. Their walls are up, even if they are coming back to you to get their second, third, or fourth vehicle. The fear of the unknown and dreaded preconceived notions will always bring them back to this stage when the conversation first starts.

What happens to that guarded feeling when I walk right up to you and tell you, "Hey, how you doing? If I can find a car you like that fits your wants and needs, can we earn your business today?"

If we're trying to move someone out of that guarded state of mind, it's not going to happen by pushing them right into a buying decision—set a budget, pick a model, walk the lot, drive the car. Making it all about me and what I can get out of you will reinforce those walls for good, and I might never break through them again.

WE HAVE TO *EARN THE RIGHT TO SELL* THEM A CAR

Our job in the first quadrant is to lower their guard. That doesn't happen with interrogation or trying to get them to commit or sniffing out whether or not they're "serious" about buying a car. It happens by putting them first.

There are people who say that customers don't want to talk about their kids or where they work—that they just want to walk in and buy a car and walk out. I see that as an excuse for not spending time getting to know the customer. I'm not asking you to drift off into rapport land. The last thing you want is to be the nicest salesperson who never sold them a car. But don't act like learning about their wants, needs, and hot buttons is the same as inviting them over for a Fourth of July barbecue.

The only way to lower a customer's guard is to get to know them. Literally meet them where they are—right there at their vehicle—and stay there. Walk around it. Ask them questions about it. Ask them open-ended questions about why they're here and what they need. Find out what compelling reasons brought them to your lot that day when they could be at an amusement park or the lake or, you know, getting a tooth filled.

This is going to surprise most customers. Most of the time, they've never experienced anything like it before. When they start to loosen up, engage in conversation, and drop some of that nervousness in favor of excitement, you know you're moving on to the next stage.

QUADRANT 2: OPEN-MINDED

We haven't eliminated everything that made our customer guarded yet. They might still be afraid of spending too much, getting the wrong car, or getting a bad deal—but now we've at least gotten to know them a little bit. We've helped them feel good about the research they've done, the decision to move on it, maybe even the trade that they've brought in. Their guard is starting to lower, and now they're willing to listen to us.

This is the "maybe I'll give you a shot" stage for the customer.

In other words, we've earned the right to do a presentation. This isn't an aimless walkaround while verbal-vomiting all over the customer with everything you know about the car—it's where we show them that we were listening and that we really are trying to help get them in the best vehicle that meets their needs.

IF WE SHOW THEM HOW MUCH WE'RE LISTENING TO THEM, THEY'LL START TO LISTEN TO US

Quadrant two is where we get to say things like "Earlier you were telling me that you needed a lot of room in the back to carry your kids' sports gear and your real estate signs—pop that hatch, let me show you the room back there."

As we paint that vehicle into their real day-to-day-life situations, they begin to believe that we're listening to their needs and that we truly do care about getting them into the right car with a good experience. Their guard is even lower now, they're open to the suggestions we have for them, and they're gaining confidence in us and in the deal.

QUADRANT 3: CONFIDENT

By this point, the pattern has been completely interrupted. We've done things completely different than anything they've experienced before. We know a good deal about them and their life, they've been involved in the presentation and demonstration that kept them as the focal point, and they've driven the vehicle and have fallen in love with it.

For thirty or forty-five minutes now, everything has been about them and their needs, and they have found the perfect car to show for it. Now they're confident that we understand them and care about their needs being met.

They're confident in our abilities and that our priorities are right.

At this point, we've earned the right to ask for the sale.

Now we can start to close with things like "You're going to love your new car. Go ahead and park it in the sold row and let's go inside to wrap it up. Are you going to be titling it in both names or just one?" We can ask for small commitments or look for objections, because we've earned the right to ask for the sale—and they can handle it—without scaring them off.

Even if they're not quite ready to make a commitment, a confident closer or salesperson will stay engaged, ask good questions, and keep having fun. Objections aren't a sign that they aren't buying—they're a sign of fear, and that's okay. On the other hand, buyers who have dropped out of confidence or maybe haven't reached it yet will say things like "I just want to know what your best price is" or "I'm going to go down the street and shop around."

Buyers who are making commitments, however big or small—parking in the sold row, coming in to talk, choosing between coffee and water—and are staying engaged have some confidence in you, and they're ready to trust you as you guide them through a win/win negotiation.

QUADRANT 4: TRUSTING

Trust isn't just given. It's earned. If we've done our job well, by the time the negotiation rolls around, we've already gotten to know the customer and lowered their guard, then we made the presentation all about them as they listened with an open mind. We reminded them that they made a great choice once they were confident that we had their best interest in mind. By the time we're ready to negotiate, it's from a place of earned trust.

On the other hand, if their objections during the negotiation center around how they don't believe you or they think you're trying to rip them off, your problem isn't in the negotiation. It's a problem that started in the first fifteen minutes of the deal. Trust isn't a checkbox that you can mark off. It's something that's built up from the moment we greet them on the lot until long after the interaction is over.

THE OUTCOME OF *THE LAST FIFTEEN* MINUTES OF THE DEAL ARE A REFLECTION OF HOW YOU HANDLED *THE FIRST FIFTEEN*

Again, I won't tell you that a buyer who comes to a point of trust will pay sticker price with a smile on their face. Trust shows up as a lagging indicator.

You might not ever get to 100 percent trust, even after you're a few cars into their trade cycle, but you're much more likely to see them again, and their guard will be down, they'll be open to your suggestions, they'll be confident in your skills, and they'll trust you more and more over time.

We're always shooting for this quadrant of trust—we're always earning the right to ask for a sale. It doesn't make negotiating easy, but it's sure as heck going to make it easi*er*. There's one more tool to understand the buyer's perspective before we can begin adapting our sales process to create win/win deals.

> Most of our time in this book will be spent on the sales process, specifically closing and negotiating. But I spend a lot of time talking about the Buyer's Quadrant and the way emotions and logic affect them (that's coming up in the next chapter). If you want to dig in a little more on these topics, head over to frictionlessnegotiating.com.

SEPARATING EMOTIONS AND LOGIC

If you're shopping around for a product and you really want to find the best price, how will you do it? Will you go right to Amazon, pick the top result, and hit "Buy Now" for two-day shipping and a one-click order? Probably not. True price shopping usually looks like multiple tabs, a bunch of searching, and double-checking reviews before finally making your purchase. Most of the time, when we're clicking through Amazon it's because we want the convenience, not the price.

Every purchase comes with its own motivation and reasoning, leading us to the Amazon-style convenience choice or the thrifty price hunt. Some people will look through fifty websites to save forty cents, while others don't think their time is worth the savings. There isn't a right or wrong type of buyer—but we need to understand what's really happening. It's not just about what they're doing, but what's happening underneath.

Every single customer, no matter what they're looking for, how they're looking for it, or whether they buy that day, uses both emotion and logic to make their decision. For a heavy researcher, speccing out the car online with the black-on-black color scheme and the twenty-inch wheels and the power ports for the kids is an *emotional* process. It's exciting and creative. But when that last page pops up with the price right there in big, bold numbers, *logic* kicks in. Now they have to figure out whether they can make it work.

Most salespeople function as that price page pop-up.

We meet the customer in their emotional state of excitement and nervousness, then immediately start asking them logical questions about their budget and expectations.

All throughout the Buyer's Quadrant, our customers are shifting between emotion and logic to inform their decisions. These are subconscious processes and dynamics that we all experience, whether or not we have the words to identify them. Before we can use the sales process to walk the buyer through the quadrants, we have to get a handle on the way emotions and logic can either work for or against us along the way.

When we talked about a guarded customer becoming even more nervous instead of more excited, that was one way to become aware of the emotions and logic of a deal. As we wrap up the buyer's journey, let's look at some other ways we can influence the right kind of emotions and only bring in logic when it's time.

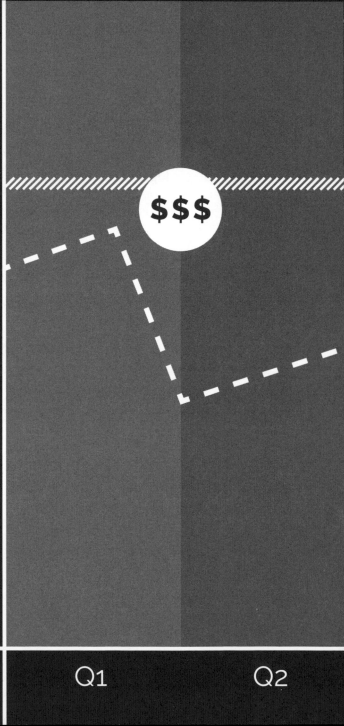

EMOTION

LOGIC

SALES PERSON

CUSTOMER

$$$

Q1

Q2

When you allow price to lead the conversation.

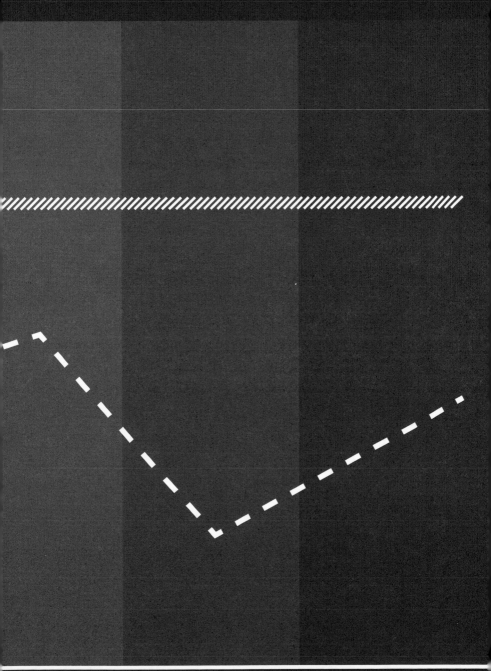

Q3   Q4   DELIVERY

EMOTIONS COME FIRST: EMPHASIZING VALUE INSTEAD OF COST

Chances are, if someone shows up at the dealership, they've already worked through some of their logical concerns around expense. That "I think it's time for a new car" discussion included the payments they could afford and the condition of their trade. They've come to a place where the emotions outweigh the logic, and they're ready to take the next step.

There's absolutely no reason for us to bring them down into logic again until the negotiation starts. In fact, our job is to get their emotion levels—excitement, anticipation, enjoyment—as high as possible, and hold them there as long as we can. Early in the process, that means our focus is on value rather than cost.

Price is 100 percent logical. It's dollars and cents, budgets and boundaries. There's no point in worrying about those details if your customer isn't completely sold. Real estate agents don't ask their buyers to submit an offer before the walkthrough, so why would we worry about numbers before they see themselves driving that specific car?

Price is reading window stickers to the customer or talking about discounts. It doesn't build any value, and it doesn't spark any positive emotions. It's just another expense that the buyer has to worry about.

Value, on the other hand, is completely emotional. It's showing the customer that the car meets their needs so well that it's actually worth more than the cost. Again, their budget is irrelevant until they can see $75,000 worth of value in a $50,000 car.

Emotion should be the only thing driving the first two quadrants as we help the buyer lower their guard and start to build their confidence up. While we're learning as much about them as we can in quadrant one, guarded, then reflecting it back to them in quadrant two, open-minded, we're validating everything that got them excited enough to come to the lot anyway. We're keeping those levels of emotion high enough to sustain them through the closing and negotiation steps still to come.

> Whether they are the spontaneous Amazon shopper or the studious researcher, they are right. Even if they picked the wrong vehicle, validate them: "It's awesome that you did your research. Let me tell you why those features are better in this other choice…" Remember, there's no wrong way to show up to a car lot. Empower the researchers and embolden the spontaneous folks and you'll keep their good emotions high.

This is the time to echo their compelling reason to show up, to direct them to the right car, and to paint that car onto the vehicle-shaped spaces on the canvas of their life. Then, in the same way that Amazon's value of convenience makes it worth the potentially higher cost, the sticker price won't matter as much. I like to say we want the customer licking the paint off the car—they've got to want to buy it more than I need to sell it.

When they can see themselves living out their day-to-day life in that vehicle by the end of the demo, their emotions will be as high as they're going to go. And if we've done our job well, they'll be at a level of excitement that will help them answer closing questions and keep that value in mind throughout the negotiation.

EMOTION

LOGIC

SALES PERSON

- - -
CUSTOMER

Q1

Q2

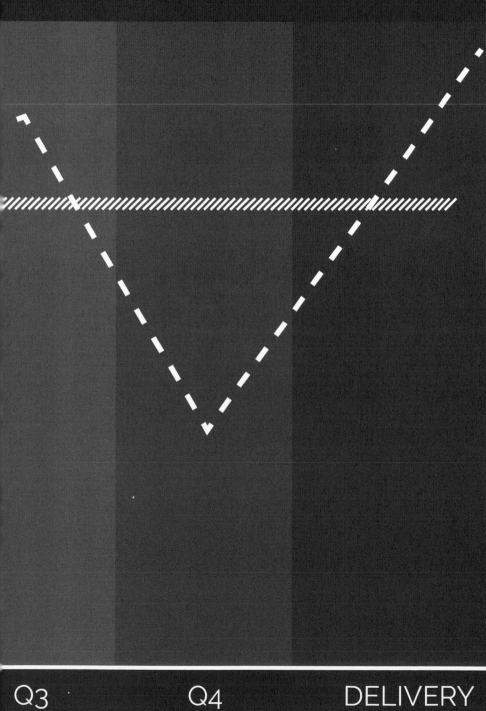

LOGIC SEALS THE DEAL: CRAFTING WIN/WIN NEGOTIATIONS

When we present the vehicle by painting it into the customer's life, it tells them something about us. We meet their open-minded willingness to listen with a genuine interest in their lives. We've heard what's important to them and made sure that the car they chose fit those parameters.

If we've done the job right, then, we'll have found the right car. After all, we're listening to them every step of the way, and if it's not the right one, they're going to let us know. To keep validating their choices and hold those levels of emotion high, we need to assume the sale. Asking them hesitant closing questions, like "Is it the right car?" introduces doubt and drops those positive emotions just when you need them to be at their highest. Because once you start getting logical, it's almost impossible to build more emotion back in.

If we understand a little bit about their life and can show them how that vehicle will make it better, they'll be much more likely to understand us as we start to shift into negotiating later on.

The challenge for salespeople is that we're naturally emotional in the first place. We're not immune to the emotions and logic in a deal—in fact, our highs are higher and our lows are lower. We have to keep our own emotions in check, especially the more negative feelings like needing the deal, being worried about the way the customer sees us, or making sure we get it right.

REMEMBER, IT'S

ENT-
HUS-
IASM

THAT SELLS CARS

Too many salespeople get caught up in a beggar's mindset, trying to do whatever they can to "earn your business." Most of us have been there in some form, and it crushes our ability to use logic. If we're asking the customer to tell us what it will take to earn their business, then they are driving the negotiation. At that level of personal emotional investment, we can't help them see their total cost of ownership, how it fits into their budget, and how gas and maintenance savings will justify the numbers. We're operating out of desperation, when more controlled emotions would leave room for inspiration.

When it's time to start talking price, the value that we build in the Pre-demo Trade Walk—the conversation that we have at the customer's car when they first show up—and during the demonstration will make all the difference. Now, they're so excited to get the car that they're helping you figure out how to fit it into their budget.

If you never introduce logic and just let them drive the negotiation, they might sign the paperwork happy, but they aren't going to drive away happy. The path of least resistance almost always leads to something like zero down for eighty-four months. It sounds great to them at the time, but you're the expert. You know that it's going to impact their trade cycle and become a liability later on when they're ready for something new. If you let them get into that loan without pushing back, once they see the drawbacks it will be too late. You might never be able to rebuild trust with that person again.

Win/lose negotiations don't always feel like a loss to the customer at the time. That's why we use logic in the late stages to help them get the best deal possible. Maybe I know that you could get a forty-eight-month lease that you could try to get out of after twenty-four or thirty months rather than five or six years for the longer loan. Maybe I can see other ways that your budget has room so that eighty-four months doesn't look so appealing. As the expert—whom you should come pretty close to trusting by this point—I'm responsible for pointing those things out as we negotiate, to steer you toward a win/win deal that will send you home happy and keep you coming back.

DRIVING HOME HAPPY

No matter what kind of purchase we wind up negotiating, don't make the mistake of thinking that signing on the dotted line ends the relationship. We want our buyer's journey to keep going after their dealership visit. That means doing our best to get them into a good deal from the get-go, then maintaining that relationship long after they've gone home.

As a manager, I've fielded calls where people told me they had a great experience until it got to the delivery.

The way you treat your buyers will stick with them. The Three-Sees delivery—*See the car? See the keys? See you later!*—keeps the buyer in that lower level of logic that the negotiation required rather than bringing them back up into a peak state of emotions and excitement when they drive off the lot in their new car.

We can't just send template emails or a string of surveys and then go radio silent until we need another sale in a few years. We have to maintain the relationship that we built during the purchase. We need to stay in touch and remain focused on their needs. Only then can we earn the right to ask for another sale when it's time to trade or end a lease.

The cycle in our industry of following the path of least resistance with the buyer and allowing them to sign on for six grand in negative equity *just so we can get a sale* has to change. I don't train people to jam buyers into suboptimal loans or to work from a place of desperation. Instead, we're training salespeople to build the best deals that we can for everyone who walks onto the lot. And to do that, we have to work with emotions and logic from the first handshake until they're gone from our lives for good.

The best way to remember the effect that emotions and logic can have on a deal is to draw it up yourself. Flip back to that chart earlier in this section and copy it onto a sticky note or a little piece of paper. Think about where your emotions are throughout the sale or when you've tried to bring in logic. Think about the way your customers show up and how they are once they're at the end of a deal. Draw it up, stick it on your desk, and remember to work on keeping those emotions as high as you can as long as you can throughout the deal.

CHAPTER 3

THE SALES PROCESS

BEFORE THE "UP"

NFL Hall of Fame receiver Marvin Harrison once said, "They pay us for practice, and the games are for fun." This kind of mentality is just one of the reasons that I use sports analogies when I'm training salespeople—not just as metaphors, but as part of our exercises too. Champions aren't made on the field or during the fight. They're great because of what they do in between. It's the same for salespeople.

What we do between customers determines our success.

It costs way too much time, money, and effort to wait until a fresh up hits the lot (first-time customer, in case you haven't used that lingo yet) before we start practicing our skills. Just talking about a technique can give you the knowledge, but turning that knowledge into a skill is where the money's at.

KNOWLEDGE + SKILLS = CONFIDENCE

Knowledge might be power in other contexts, but for our industry it's dangerous all by itself. A lot of people know a lot of things, but few of them are doing anything about it. In chapter 1, we talked about the process of turning new information into your own new skill by recognizing that it works, internalizing its technique, then customizing it to make it your own. The only way to internalize something is to practice it over and over again, by yourself or with your coworkers, until it comes out sounding natural, like you're just having a conversation.

Knowledge doesn't become a skill until it's just what you do without thinking about it. It's not you closing. It's not you negotiating. It's just what comes naturally to you right when you need it, like a reflex.

Reading a script over and over again or role-playing with someone on the sales floor is not fun. Even though I love to refer to sports, we differ on this point. Practice before the game can be a little bit fun. Practicing a script out loud by yourself is boring, mundane, repetitive work and not at all rewarding in the moment. But if you want to be great, you have to have the intestinal fortitude to power through that boredom of practice.

We're living in the most educated and most distracted society that has ever existed. We have to work that much harder to set the phone down, tune out the world, and do the unrewarding work in between customers.

If you can do that, your knowledge will turn into valuable, instinctual skills that will ultimately raise your confidence and change the way you interact with everyone on your lot.

GET YOUR ATTITUDE RIGHT

Before you talk to the next up, make sure your head is right and you're ready to go. That means believing that a customer walking onto the lot is ready to buy a new vehicle, *now*. We don't get to prejudge whether someone is "serious" or not. They drove all the way over, fully expecting to invest two, three, four hours of their life in us. We owe it to them to give them all we've got.

Thinking about that emotions and logic chart, our emotions start off just as high as the customer's, if not higher. While there's always going to be some level of nervousness involved, we can't have high emotions that are also negative.

ALWAYS DO A **CHECK-UP** *FROM THE* **NECK UP** *BEFORE YOU TAKE YOUR* **NEXT UP**

Maybe you just spent three hours with someone on a Saturday morning, and they were a jackass and left without buying. Four hours later, that guy is at Chuck E. Cheese eating pizza and playing Skee-Ball with his kid and couldn't pick you out of a lineup, while you're left on the lot pissing and moaning about how ridiculous he was, transferring that negativity to the next up and costing yourself money. Where is your mindset? What kind of emotions do you have?

If you've got a bad attitude, you'll blow customers off the lot and cost yourself potentially thousands of dollars in commission. That energy will rub off on everyone you talk to and will waste all of your time. We're in the people business before the car business, so if we can't set our attitude first, we might as well step back until we can try again from a better place.

The sales process isn't something that we do *to* a customer. The sales process is what we do *for* them. Having the right mindset keeps us focused on the buyer and their needs, so that we can understand before being understood, meet them where they are, and help guide them through the Buyer's Quadrant.

The hardest part of all of this is doing it. It's one thing to think you understand once you've heard it or read it, and it's something totally different to practice it until you can't do anything else. Take a look at your calendar right now. When can you squeeze in time to practice good closings or run through the sales process in your mind or with a buddy? Commit to making it part of your everyday routine—that fifteen to twenty minutes is worth thousands in commissions!

THE SALES QUADRANT

The old-school sales process, even if it wasn't recognizable as a process, almost always included talking about budget, wandering the lot talking about features and sticker prices, doing multiple demos, walking their trade in a silent walkaround, then going inside to "see what we can do for you," even if we weren't completely sure the customer had decided on that vehicle. It took hours, didn't always end in a sale, and put a bad taste in everyone's mouth.

Today, time is everyone's most valuable commodity. One of the common complaints that customers offer in surveys is that it took too long to buy their car. There are a lot of reasons people hate buying cars, but that one turns up over and over again. No one wants to take five hours to buy a car—and there's no reason that they should.

When I got back on the sales floor after only doing trainings for so many years, I realized there were a lot of steps we could layer and rearrange to make the process shorter and easier for everyone. There's no reason to wander the lot without knowing anything about the person or what they want. There's no reason to wait until the end to do the appraisal—it doesn't cost anything, and it adds value right away. There's no reason to do a silent walkaround, making the customer feel defensive just before we sit down to negotiate.

TIME
IS THE NEW CURRENCY. USE IT WISELY

As we started to layer the steps of the sale together, we realized we had found a sales process that cuts through a lot of the problems both customers and salespeople run into.

Any and every successful person has a repeatable process for everything that they do. From the clothes that they wear to the way they practice their skills to their routines at work or on the field, they aren't winging it. There is a process to follow, and when something doesn't go right, they can identify the error or flaw and work to get better at it.

I believe car sales should follow a repeatable process as well. It should be quick, efficient, and a pattern interrupt that can be used with every single customer. Incidentally, I also believe that the Buyer's Quadrant gives us clues as to how that process should go.

This is the process that I train people on now, not just from a hotel conference room, but side by side with them on the sales floor. We've adapted it and optimized it, always looking to stay ahead of the curve to meet the customer where they are. My goal with this process is to move the buyer through their quadrants and get them all the way to finance within an hour to an hour and fifteen minutes from the time they walked onto the lot.

SALES QUADRANT

(BUYERS QUADRANT)

1	**2**
REASSURE THE CUSTOMER (GUARDED)	**HIGH-IMPACT PRESENTATION** (OPEN-MINDED)
3	**4**
TRANSITION THE CUSTOMER (CONFIDENT)	**WIN/WIN TRANSACTION** (TRUST)

QUADRANT 1: REASSURE THE CUSTOMER

(THE PRE-DEMO TRADE WALK)

Even though there's some compelling, often exciting reason that someone sets out to buy a car, their emotions are running high with anxiety and fear as well. They're worried about getting a bad deal or overspending, so their guard is up. We need to reassure them that this experience is going to be different. We can't just tell them that we mean well—we have to show them.

Instead of going straight from the greeting at the curb to the lot like they expect, go to their vehicle and get to know them. That's their safety bubble and where they're more likely to open up to you. Show them that this is going to be all about them by letting them know that you'll get them an appraisal on their vehicle, whether they buy a car from you or not. Learn who they are and what they're looking for. Ask them what type of driving they do, what they love about their vehicle, and what they don't like that they want to change for the next one. Ask them what kind of research they've done and what brought them out to the lot.

If you ask open-ended questions, it not only gives you more information, but it empowers them as well. They become the salesperson, telling you everything you need to know to sell them a car.

This is what I call the Sales Quadrant.

Before, this step came later in the process and was called the Silent Walkaround. We walked around the car, touched dents and dings, put pennies in the tire tread, made interesting noises, and jotted things down. The whole time, customers would defend the things we spotted, panicking about what it all meant. This eliminated all their excitement and raised their defenses just before they sat down to start the biggest pressure point of the deal—the negotiation.

Our lives are in our cars, and as you walk around your customer's car you'll get clues about who they are. Their bumper stickers, bike racks, and tow hitches tell you who they are and give you common ground for conversation. The way they talk about their current car will tell you what they want and why they want it—and they'll absolutely talk about it, because everyone wants to get the most out of their trade. They'll become the salesperson as they talk their current vehicle up, and it will tell you a lot about them as well.

As you gather this information, some of it will help you do a better presentation, while some of it—like the scan of the driver's license and trade VIN—will go right into your CRM to speed up the back end of the deal later on. Conversations about the condition of their vehicle can get you a jump on trade valuation, and mileage and maintenance conversations tell if you'll be able to do a Gas Savings or Maintenance Close when the time comes—more on that later in the book.

All the while, you've completely interrupted the pattern that they've experienced before. Stay close to their "home base," like we all had playing childhood games of tag, and they will feel safe, surprised, and delighted as you encourage them, validate their excitement, and get them ready to meet their new car.

> Goal for the Pre-demo Trade Walk: Fifteen minutes
>
> Keys to remember: stay close to their car, input any applicable data into the CRM on your mobile device right then, ask open-ended questions, then shut up and listen.

QUADRANT 2: CREATE MENTAL OWNERSHIP (HIGH-IMPACT PRESENTATION)

In the Pre-demo Trade Walk, we're painting their life onto a blank canvas. We're walking around their car, collecting all of the information they can give us, and piecing it together to see what their life is like. Their guard should be lower by that point, and we'll find the right vehicle to present—so we can begin painting it into the canvas of their life.

We've been trained to memorize all of the specs about our

vehicles, but none of that matters if it won't matter to the customer. To disrupt the pattern here, everything about the presentation should connect with a need, want, and hot button of theirs from what you learned in quadrant one.

> Start with the least expensive vehicle in the inventory that closest fits their wants, needs, and hot buttons. You can always go up, but if you start high and have to drop down, negotiation is going to be tough.

When we make it to negotiation skills later in the book, you'll see one of the Golden Rules of Negotiation is that "whoever appears to care least about a deal, wins." By showing them the car that best meets their needs, then only talking about it in those terms, we keep it about them and how much they need the car—not how cool we think it is and how badly we want to sell it.

Tell-arounds—where we walk in circles around the vehicle and tell the customer everything we can think of—don't do anything except raise the cost. There's no mental ownership for value, just a constant *cha-ching* as you list off features. Unfortunately, most of us have been trained to memorize lists of specs, and practice makes permanent. To change the way we present vehicles, we have to practice in between customers until our instincts become better.

This is where you can get them to see their furniture in the house before they've made an offer. It's where you build $75,000 in value for a $50,000 car:

> *Earlier, you told me how you have to launch your boat by yourself a lot. This truck has an all new back-up camera with hitch assist. So what that means to you is that it'll make launching and pulling your boat out of the water a lot easier, not to mention it'll keep you from dinging the bumper or folding the license plate in half. I know you said that was important to you; wouldn't that be nice to have?*

***

> *Remember telling me you needed more room in the back for your real estate signs and all the kids' gear? Pop that latch and let me show you how much room's in there.*

I train people to do a three-point walkaround presentation: on the lot, do one FAB at each of the three points on the outside of the vehicle based on the customer's hot buttons, then a few FABs inside. After that, you go on a demo drive, where "the feel of the wheel seals the deal." Have a preplanned stopping point where you do another three-point walkaround and, if there are two drivers, have a second stopping point where you focus your FABs on the second driver. The max should only ever be nine FABs. That's it.

By this point, they should see so much value in that vehicle that they start to take mental ownership of it. They see it in their life so clearly that they can't imagine not getting it.[2]

The gross that we make on the deal can be traced back to this step. If the value climbs higher than the price during the presentation/demonstration, they're going to want you to help them fit it into their budget, not the other way around.

When everything that we do is about them, their confidence only grows throughout the process. Then, when it's time to close, you've earned the right to ask for the sale. Everything we do at each step affects the rest of them. If you have challenges in your negotiation, often it circles back to this step and the fact that the customer doesn't see the value based on the price.

Goal for the presentation/demonstration: Twenty minutes

Keys: create mental ownership, stay focused on them, "whoever appears to care least about the deal wins."

---

2   Notice I didn't say "buying" it—this is something that I try to work with my students on. Even Apple is moving away from the word "buy." Getting focuses on what they have gained (emotional), while buying focuses on the expense (logical).

QUADRANT 3: TRANSITION THE CUSTOMER

(CLOSE THE SALE OR FLUSH OUT OBJECTIONS)

The end of the demo is the highest emotional point of the sale. Now, if you're stiff and bowed up or nervous and unsure, that customer is going to mirror your demeanor and make this awkward and difficult. But assuming you've internalized and customized your closes, they'll mirror your conversational and confident tone.

Once you're back on the lot, assuming this statement is true, you might say something like "This seems like the perfect car for you. Park it over in the sold row and we'll go inside and wrap it up. Are you guys going to both be on the title or will it just be one of you?"

If you did a good job in the other quadrants, their excitement might be enough, and they'll just answer you. Did the close just work? *Yes!*

They might also let logic and fear kick in, and they'll say, "Woah, pump the brakes..." and give you an objection. Did the close just work? *Again, yes!*

A GOOD INITIAL CLOSE *WILL ALWAYS* SECURE A COMMITMENT – *OR* – FLUSH OUT AN OBJECTION

The objective of a close is to either get a commitment on the car or flush out an objection. Both outcomes are helpful. Bad closing questions are all about the numbers or begging for a deal, while a good closing question isn't even designed to close the sale necessarily. It's to secure commitments or flush out objections that we can overcome to secure that commitment.

People are going to object. If we've done a great job in the first two quadrants and have internalized and customized closing techniques (more on that later in the book), then we can overcome those objections and get down to the sale.

You don't have to answer their objections directly to overcome them either. Remember that they're reflex responses and often more about fear rather than specific details at this point—almost like the customer slides back down to a guarded quadrant one. Reassuring them that you still have their interests in mind is often enough. For example, if they object that they aren't sure they can afford it, validate their concern:

I understand. It just sounds like you're on a budget, am I right?

Customer: Yeah.

So other than us sitting down and fitting this into your budget, is there any other reason we couldn't wrap it up?

Customer: We just want to make sure we can afford it.

That's the easiest part of my job. Let's go inside and finish this up, so you guys can start enjoying your new car. Did you both want to be on the title, or just one of you?

As a salesperson, my job is to validate that this is the right car for you and that I'm here to help make this transition simple and smooth. Closing is not a single step, but a process—and a high-stress one at that. While there is a formal closing question, there are lots of little actions and answers that continue to confirm the sale or flush out further objections, so that when you make it to the negotiation, both you and the customer are sure that they are ready to buy.

The last thing you want is to start the next step without getting a commitment—if you don't, you'll just be negotiating with yourself.

> Goal for the Formal Close: Fifteen minutes
>
> Keys to remember: practice your closing strategies, be prepared to overcome their objections, ride the emotional high from the demo.

QUADRANT 4: WIN/WIN TRANSACTION

(EARN THEIR TRUST AND NEGOTIATE FOR GROSS)

Historically, we have been told that speed kills on the lot. I believe that is outdated. Ultimately, slow kills with today's buyer. Once we get a commitment from the customer and they're demonstrating confidence and even a little trust, the clock is ticking. They're as emotional as they'll ever get at the end of quadrant two, and as you move through quadrant three, now logic starts to take over as they approach the negotiation.

They're thinking about their payments, internet reports, all that research, and getting a good deal. Our job is to justify all of that. We have to make the numbers make sense. If we did our job up to this point, there's a lot of emotions to draw from. If not, it becomes stressful and difficult. We begin to negotiate out of fear and desperation, begging to earn their business instead of demonstrating things that will reinforce their trust.

When we can pull from all of the information we gathered during the Pre-demo Trade Walk, then build on all of the value we created during the presentation/demonstration and the commitment we just got while closing, negotiation can actually be fun. Working the numbers becomes a way to make that perfect vehicle fit into the customer's budget.

Amateurs let the customer drive the negotiation. They ask what needs to happen to make it work, then bounce back and forth between the customer and manager or finance department until some sort of deal can be ground out. This isn't even negotiation at all—it's being an offer presenter, and it's exhausting for everyone.

Professional negotiators, which anyone can become, are creative. They're working toward a win/win scenario that sets a foundation for every other car deal that will happen with that customer.

We're still working to keep their guard low. We're still demonstrating that we care about them, encouraging them to keep an open mind to hear what we're suggesting. We're still building their confidence and trust in us, and we're still securing commitments throughout the process. But all of that work leading up to this point can be lost with a bad negotiation approach.

If we ask the customer to tell us their numbers first, we're going to lose their emotional high and our advantage in the negotiation. If we're hesitant or not confident ourselves, we're going to lose their confidence in us.

Start the negotiation yourself. Be confident in your expertise—you know your product, and now you know your customer. You can make this work better than they could on their own, so there's no reason to ask them to be the expert and tell you how they think it should go.

Open it up with the best way to buy a car, with plenty of built-in room to come down—whether that's in the price, trade, down, or payment structures. If they choose that best way, congratulations, that's great for you and them. If we need to come down on our numbers, it'll feel like victories that make the negotiation fun for them and successful for you.

A good deal for the customer is one that *feels* good. When we make sure our process follows their natural path toward trust, and when we work with their emotional and logical inclinations, we could make $5,000 on the deal and they'll still feel like they won. Value always wins over price, which means a great sale is about creating a great experience while getting them in their ideal vehicle.

> Goal for negotiating: Thirty minutes
>
> Keys to remember: build on the trust and value that you've created to this point; negotiate from a position of strength; be creative and have fun.

If you're counting, that's just a little over an hour accounted for in our timeline. You might go a little bit over, but the days of five-hour car deals have to be over. We're not wandering the lot looking at a hundred different cars or dumping needless data on them. That's what Six-Car Steve does, and his presentation could put a cup of coffee to sleep! We're not waiting until the end to hand-write all of the trade information. We're using technology, layering steps, and staying efficient in our presentations.

Most importantly, if we have built the value higher than the price in the first two quadrants and secured a clear commitment in the third, negotiation is going to go a hell of a lot faster than it typically would. By separating the commitment from the discussion around numbers, we can more easily avoid the slow grind that wears us all down.

Are you counting? That's just over an hour from beginning to end. Try this exercise: think back on your last sale or set the timer on your next one. How much time are you spending at each step? Total? How much happier would your customers be if you could knock that down by half or better? I'm not saying it will happen every time, but I can tell you that these are ways we get close to that target just about every time.

SEPARATING CLOSING FROM NEGOTIATING

Coming up in the car business, I was taught *ABC: Always Be Closing*, but I wasn't taught what that really meant. I thought it was one step, not two; to me closing was negotiating and negotiating was closing. We think of closing as the thing that we do at the very end to complete the sale. Closing was throwing a bunch of numbers at them to try to get a commitment and hoping there would be gross left over after the grind.

In reality, these are very different functions with a very specific order.

Asking, "You want to go inside and see what we can do for you?" doesn't tell us whether or not they are committed. It tells us (and them!) that we're willing to go drop the price and drop the price until we take a loss and they ring a bell. That's not negotiating—it's a slow grind that nobody likes.

The formal closing question is about getting a commitment before the numbers are even a factor. It should come after the demo, when emotions are highest and that sense of value is clear. If we miss that step, then we wind up negotiating for a car deal rather than negotiating for gross.

A good negotiation is working out the total cost of ownership and fitting it into their budget. It's figuring out how the payments that are $125 more per month than what they have now actually work out in their total monthly outlay. It's bringing what you know about the customer from the Pre-demo Trade Walk back around to help make it work. While little closing techniques show up throughout the negotiation to hold their commitment, none of that works if you're still trying to get them to commit to the car itself.

Once I learned to separate closing and negotiating, I could sit down at the table with people who had already decided to buy the car, and I just had to figure out how much I was going to make on the deal.

NEGOTIATING IS WHEN WE MAKE THE CUSTOMER FEEL LIKE THEY'VE WON

REVISITING EMOTIONS AND LOGIC

Every step of a car deal is rooted in either emotions or logic, and closing and negotiation aren't any different. Not only should they be separated as steps, but they are separate functions all on their own: closing is emotional, and negotiating is logical.

No one is ever 100 percent logical or 100 percent emotional, but the levels will always be affected by the process and will affect the process. If the value is high, those emotions will hang on through the negotiation to balance out some of the logic. If price comes up too early, that logic will weigh them down and keep the emotions lower than it could have been.

There's always the hard-ass who is as logical as you can get. It's going to happen. But that's the minority. We're training for the majority of people who just want to get their car without any more hassle than necessary.

If we start price conversations too early, we force the customer to come down from their emotions and become logical. We might still be able to get them a little excited when they finally drive the car, but it won't ever be at the level that it would have been if we had met them in their excitement and kept them there until the last possible minute.

What's worse, when we force that logic and give them the option to tell us a number early on, when we sit down at the table and lay their $300 per month target out against the $778 per month reality, any trust we had built will be broken. Even if they buy a car, they won't be happy about it and they won't trust us enough to come back.

Get the commitment when their emotions are high, and you've earned the right to ask for the sale. Wait to work the negotiation until there's enough excitement, value, confidence, and trust in place to counteract the logic and concerns.

> Don't forget to keep your own emotions in check. For the salesperson, even the negotiation is filled with emotion. We don't want to blow the sale—but wanting it too much can actually be what kills it. Stay customer-focused from beginning to end, and that will help keep your excitement, eagerness, and fears in check.

THE RIPPLE EFFECT OF GOOD PRACTICES

If you could rewind an entire day's worth of deals with a GoPro on the sales team, you would see that the ones who were laughing and having fun, who got the customer to like them, and who stayed focused on the task at hand are also the ones who find the most success. The salespeople who you see trying to grind out a deal by starting with price and a vague, "If I can give you a great deal, can I earn your business?" will be miserable and unsuccessful, even if the customer takes delivery at the end of the day.

The very first things that you do with a customer—connecting with them and keeping those emotions high—are like tossing a pebble into a pond. The ripple effect through the rest of the sales process can move you toward a win/win negotiation or push you into a mess.

When customers come onto the lot, they're closer to being excited and emotional than they are to being fully logical. Our goal is to keep them there as long as possible, so that when logic kicks in during the negotiation, they're ready for it. In the first two quadrants, we're finding out everything we can about the person and getting the value and excitement as high as possible, then leveraging those emotions in closing so we can better handle the logic drift when we're negotiating at the end.

If we ask good questions, engage, and actively listen to learn exactly what they want—not just the car they think they want but the car that meets their needs—then we earn the right to make suggestions. We earn the right to point them toward a different car, suggest other options, and get creative to make the car fit in their budget. The way we approach those first conversations in quadrants one and two determines the freedom we have in quadrants three and four.

By the time we make it to the negotiation, we should be able to capitalize on the ripples that we set into motion back in the very beginning. We got to know the customer, educated them on their trade, painted the vehicle into their lives, built the value up beyond the actual price but stayed off of numbers so that we could start the negotiation at the right time, kept their emotions up, and gained a commitment by eliminating all other options. Now we get to talk numbers. Now we get to build in wins. Now we get to have fun helping them get the car that they've already taken mental ownership of.

Remember, no matter what the actual numbers say about the deal, it's the entire experience that the customer will remember. If they didn't feel heard, understood, and cared about all the way through, you're going to run into problems in the negotiation and have a less than happy customer at the end of the deal. But if you're having fun helping them get what they want, the emotions win the day.

> *Enthus-i-a-s-m sells cars: I Am Sold Myself.* Believe from the top of your head to the bottom of your toes that if they don't buy the car from you, it'll be the biggest mistake of their life. Assume the sale, assume the win, and bring them along for the ride.

THE 3R's

1. *RESPOND*
2. *REASSURE*
3. *REDIRECT*

BYPASSING: THE GLUE OF THE SALES PROCESS

Once we're ready to separate closing and negotiating and delay them until their proper place in the process, it might be frustrating when customers show up wanting to talk price first. But that's just what we've trained them to do. Every time we greet someone on the lot with "What are you looking to spend?" we're reinforcing habits around price-focused car deals. If we're going to change that, we have to condition the buyers as much as ourselves. This is a practice called bypassing, and it's the glue that holds the whole thing together if we're going to be successful at closing and negotiating.

When they start talking about their budget and getting the best price, it's our job to bypass that conversation until it's time for it. The art of bypassing is one of the most underrated skills that a great negotiator has. It is the glue that keeps the sales process intact so that we're able to start the negotiation once we have a clear commitment, rather than letting the customer start it early on.

For a payment question, bypassing might sound something like "That'll actually depend on the trim level and equipment you ultimately choose. Did you want basic transportation or something loaded that the whole family can enjoy?"

YOU BUILD VALUE ON YOUR FEET AND TALK PRICE ON YOUR SEAT

Even if someone comes in very aggressively wanting to talk price, the integrity of the sales process matters. Don't get stressed—trust your preparation and bypass the price conversation until it's time: "We didn't get to be the best dealer by having the worst prices. That's the easiest part of my job, let's make sure we have the right car for you, and we'll definitely take care of you on the price. Will this be more for city driving and errands or highway driving and commuting?"

Bypassing keeps closing and negotiating separate, and it's a practice that starts in the very beginning of the interaction. Every time they want to drop into logic and numbers, respond to their concerns, reassure them that you will get them all the information they need and you have their best interests in mind, and then redirect them to the stage of the sales process that you're in.

Their concern doesn't go away, but we set it aside to buy time until we can get the value higher than the price. If we get into a price conversation within the first five minutes, the entire sales process falls apart. Emotions and logic go off course, the buyer is still guarded, and we haven't had time to set up a proper negotiation.

Price should be the last thing that we talk about, not the first.

Bypassing can be tricky if you haven't practiced. The difference between a confident bypass and a hesitation can change the customer's perception of you. The only way to get better is to do it over and over again. I have some bypassing tools for you to work on later in the book and on frictionlessnegotiating.com.

PART II

FRICTIONLESS CLOSING

CHAPTER 4

CLOSE FOR VOLUME

RE-DEFINING CLOSING

When I started in this business back in 1990, I was lucky enough to get some training around a sales process I could follow. It worked for its time—it was at least a repeatable process, and it carried me for eleven years, all the way from lot guy to the general manager. After I graduated from NADA Academy back in 2000, I started training people on the industry's standard process. Again, it wasn't bad and at least it was a process, but we developed everything from a distance. I was teaching theories from hotels, not actually testing them in the field.

When I went back to run a Ford store after thirteen years, I realized that what we had been teaching was good—but it was out of touch with the way buyers had changed. For example, we taught that "speed kills on the lot," when in reality, the biggest complaint anyone had was about how long it took to buy a car. Our entire process was out of order and took way too long.

I had been teaching tens of thousands of people how to do things that, in my eyes, were now wrong or, at the very least, not the most efficient and customer friendly.

Once I got back on the lot and could see what was and wasn't working, I started to tackle some of our biggest hang-ups from the combined perspective of a trainer, manager, and salesperson. Most of our time monsters got sorted out by layering the sales process and rearranging our approach. As we changed the way we did the walkaround and how we did our presentations, the first half of the sales quadrant started to take shape. But then there was still this big block of time that would get eaten up at the end, when it was time to actually wrap up the sale.

We'd bring them inside after doing a silent walkaround, set them down, fill out an appraisal slip, get the manager to finish the appraisal, and complete the paperwork—all before starting the negotiation. Two hours of back-and-forth after the presentation ended, we might or might not have a deal. Moving the trade walk and appraisal to the beginning helped speed up the velocity of the deal, and so did cutting down the presentation/demonstration time, while utilizing technology throughout the process.

But we were still grinding out the deal to the end, and it was killing the whole process.

The solution came to me when I was holding in-house training at a dealership. I was coaching the managers while they were working deals, and the whole time I was there, practically every deal that came to the desk was blowing up. We quickly realized that the managers were getting involved too late in every deal and as a result, it took a ton of time. All of it came down to one common thread: the customer wasn't committed. Managers getting involved was a good thing—the problem was that it was after the first pencil and often too late to deliver a win/win situation.

Finally, I realized we had to leave the office and get out there with them. Before any penciling happened, we needed to sit down with the customer ourselves to find out how committed they really were.

Just as I suspected, the salespeople had become customer advocates—closer to being sales-prevention people than actually trying to make deals happen. They didn't want to "close" them and didn't want to pressure people, so they were bringing half-hearted commitments into the negotiation, hoping that the right number would make it work.

As soon as we made sure the customer was committed

first, or at least what their level of commitment was, the entire negotiation process became faster and more efficient. Now, I train all of my managers to do this Pre-Negotiation Interview to make sure the negotiating stage is set up properly.

The first step is understanding what it really means to get that commitment in the first place. Let's make sure we're clear on what closing is first, because not getting it right can come back to bite us at the end of the deal.

BYPASSING AND THE RIGHT TIME TO ASK FOR THE SALE

In the previous chapters, we said that a good closing question will get the commitment or flush out an objection. One mistake that we tend to make early on is assuming that the customer is objecting when they ask about the price, so we jump right into figuring out how to close the deal. Even though we're still doing the presentation or are even in the Pre-demo Trade Walk, we feel obligated to start making concessions the second the customer says, "What's your best price?"

That person is about to make one of the biggest investments of their life—of course they *want* to know what the best price is. But there's no point in you telling them that price before they even know they like the vehicle. If you want to get them past their concerns, you need to bypass the numbers discussion until you've built value and earned their confidence in the other quadrants, because that's what they really need. Technically, the customer can't give you an objection to buying until you ask them to buy.

If we chase early questions about price, we'll start making promises and offers at the wrong stage of the deal. The customer will have triggered the negotiation phase before anything else has been completed, and, as we'll see later on, whoever starts the negotiation has the advantage.

Bypassing—avoiding negotiating in the first fifteen or so minutes of the deal so you can be the one to start in the last fifteen—keeps the sales process intact. It moves the conversation about price until it's the right time in the deal to ask for the sale. We begin the closing phase when emotions and value are high and we've earned the right to ask for the sale. Then we can overcome their objections to gain a commitment on the vehicle and set up a successful negotiation.

CLOSING IS A SERIES OF ACTIONS, ANSWERS, AND EVENTS THAT ELIMINATE ALL OTHER OPTIONS

CLOSING IS HIGHLY EMOTIONAL

Stopping ourselves from talking price and trying to nego-tiate early is challenging, and it can be even more difficult to make ourselves ask direct closing questions when it's time. If we're bold enough to ask for the sale at all, we instinctively wait until the last possible minute—and resort to our reflexes and poor closing questions out of fear. That's because closing is highly emotional.

The commitment to buy is driven by the same emotional energy that compelled them to show up on the lot with the intention to buy—both the excitement and the ner-vousness—but on a much higher level. The longer they're there, the more their emotions build up. And ours are just as high. We're afraid that we'll say or do something to lose this deal we've been working so hard to seal.

Instead of leveraging the excitement, all too often we give in to the nervousness and fears and just run away. We avoid asking for a commitment at all.

The problem with that is, at some point, the buyer has to commit to *buying*. If we make closing and negotiation one big, bulky, combined process, then we're negotiating for the sale, not for gross. On our end, we'll wind up taking a loss and a hit on the CSI. From the buyer's perspective, we're talking them into something, not helping it fit into their life. It's lose/win at best, lose/lose more often.

While closing is an emotionally driven step that should come at the most emotional point of the deal, it doesn't have to be dramatic or scary. That's why we wait until quadrant three to do it—after the demo, when they're in love with the car and see it painted into their lives, and when we believe from the top of our head to the bottom of our toes that they need that car.

By then, we know they love the car and they know we're looking out for them. They're behind the wheel and can see that car being part of their life. If we did a good job to that point, then they've already taken mental ownership anyway. We're just confirming it. We're finding out *how* they want to own it, not *if*.

THE FEEL OF THE WHEEL SEALS THE DEAL

CLOSING IS A PROCESS, NOT A STEP

We've all heard this saying, and it is true. Just like we have to work to keep the customer's guard down even after they've moved onto their second and third quadrants and are starting to trust us, we also have to keep closing throughout the negotiation. But we can't let that become an excuse to never ask for the sale. The ultimate goal is to have a committed customer before you negotiate, and that can only happen if you ask a clear initial closing question.

Remember, closing is about getting a commitment from the customer. We need to know they're committed to buying, and we need to help them remember that commitment until the deal is done.

The initial closing question locks in their emotional response to the car, and that's what fuels a good negotiation. You've created $75,000 worth of value in a $50,000 car. They're behind the wheel and more in love with it than they thought they would be when it first caught their eye. They're at your store on their day off, intending to buy a car, and this is the car they want to buy. Now is the time to get them to say it.

Keep your questions conversational and simple. It's easier to decide whether you want the title in one name or two than it is to commit to going inside to see what $70,000 looks like in monthly payments on a piece of paper. It's easier to park the car in the sold row or to decide to have coffee instead of water than it is to decide right there on the lot if you're ready to spend the money.

In most cases, I don't believe you'll obtain a 100 percent commitment from the customer.

Sure, the guy with a 420 credit score might be 100 percent committed if you can get him approved—but most customers can walk away from the deal at any point. Moving the customer from "we like the car" to "we're committed to getting it" comes down to a series of actions, answers, and events that eliminate all other options.

Again, it's not about *if*—do you want the car, would you like the car, is this the car for you—but *how* they want to own it. If they tell you how they want to own it, they're committed. If they want to pump the brakes, they have objections that you need to flush out. Overcome their true objections, buy time for just a little bit longer, and go in for the commitment again until there's no option but to wrap it up at the negotiation table.

> This phase of the deal never gets enough love. Think back over your last five interactions with a customer. Can you identify clear closing questions that you asked them? Where were their emotion levels when you asked? How did they respond? How did the deal go after that? If you didn't ask a clear closing question, what did that do to the deal?

OVERCOMING YOUR OWN OBJECTIONS

Fear is the biggest challenge that most salespeople face in getting a commitment from a customer. I believe it comes from a lack of confidence in their ability. If you're not practicing before you get in front of the customer, or you don't know what to practice at all, there's no way to be confident that it's going to sound good or that it will work. If you've skipped steps early on in the sales process, there's no way to be confident that it's the right car for the customer and that they want it.

It happens to the best of us—whether we're brand-new or veterans. We don't know, we don't practice, or we don't stick to process, and then we feel stuck at the end.

That's when some of the worst closing questions you can think of start to pop up:

I'm one car away from hitting my goal. Will you guys please help me out today? (The Beggar's Close.)

I don't want to pressure you, but is this a car you might consider? (Weaker than circus lemonade!)

If I can make you a great deal, will you buy it? (Commits you, not the customer.)

For anyone who started in car sales after the recession, it's possible that these are the only kinds of closing questions you've heard or used. You might not even be able to identify a close in most conversations. And that approach might've even worked for you and the people around you. Just know that it only worked in spite of these habits, not because of them.

No matter your background, this is a problem for our entire industry: instead of learning the right sales process and having the discipline to stick with it 100 percent of the time, we say and do things early on that come back to bite us in the closing and negotiation steps.

To try to make up for what we don't know, we take shortcuts that don't work and pick up habits that don't serve us or the customer. Then we dread those closing and negotiation steps the next time, so we cut even more corners...

That ripple effect that we talked about isn't always positive. Sometimes it makes a mess.

It's not that we don't want to sell cars or spend time with people anymore. We're just tired of grinding out uncommitted deals, and unless we get some better tools in our toolboxes, it's not going to get any easier.

In other words, the biggest challenge around getting a commitment from the customer isn't about the customer at all. It's how we approach it from the beginning. It's overcoming our own lack of confidence, and fear is what holds us back from realizing our true potential.

EMBRACING CHANGE

Let's be real here: change is tough. Some people embrace it, but most people run from it or fight it. Change is scary enough that we can go years without asking, "Why do we do it that way?" Dealerships hang on to old, outdated ways of working deals just because that's the way things have always been done.

It reminds me of someone I work with who owned a dealership for years. He told us that a new General Motors rep came in one day through the service entrance and asked him, "Hey, when did you start running a prison?"

Confused, he followed the rep out to the customer entrance.

"Let me show you this," the guy told him, and pointed to a solid steel door with a four-by-six window that had bars through it. "That's what customers enter through when they come to your dealership."

It looked like solitary confinement, and it had been there for years without anyone noticing. Why *did* they have that door? No one knew. It was just the door that had always been there.

So why do we try to negotiate without getting a clear commitment first? No one really knows. It's just the way we've always done it. It doesn't make us bad, necessarily—but it sure as hell doesn't make us good. The only question is whether we're willing to learn something new. We've got to overcome our own objections to selling, being direct, and actually closing the customer if we want to have a career in sales.

Embrace change or become extinct, right? If I could adapt after twenty-plus years of doing it the old way, anyone can learn to do it better.

The way that I was taught to sell cars might have had some underlying structure, but by the time we got to closing and negotiation, it was a mess. We would take any sort of commitment at all, then throw them in a room and gang up on them to try to close the deal. We'd grind it out until it was done, no matter what. We had the *"win at all costs"* mentality.

No one wants to change. It's uncomfortable and difficult. But if we don't change, our whole industry might wind up in a museum one day, an extinct spectacle.

Honestly, we can bring it in even closer than that. Maybe you won't see the day when car sales are completely automated, but what's your expense right now? What are the ripples of bad deals costing you? Maybe you're not getting the sales you need. Maybe the customers are having a bad experience, so they walk away from a deal without any loyalty to you at all and no desire to come back to buy another car from you.

On the other hand, after training thousands of salespeople, managers, and dealers to embrace change and adapt to the new world, I know what kind of success waits on the other side. Once you finally internalize it, you'll wonder why you ever did things the way you used to.

SEVEN WAYS TO CHANGE THE WAY YOU CLOSE

1. Your belief and your attitude will determine your success. You might be good now, but good is great's biggest enemy. Relax, get into a great mindset, and the rest will follow.

2. Always ask for the sale. It sounds silly on paper, but few salespeople actually do it. You are a salesperson, not the buyer's agent or someone taking orders. You're there to close, so do it.

3. Be direct. With the first two quadrants done, you can be sure it's the perfect car for them—so tell them. Stay relaxed and conversational, but validate their decision to buy that car.

4. Reassure the customer and validate their decision. In that thirty-second battle after the demo, everyone is nervous. Refer back to what you learned about them in the Pre-demo Trade Walk and presentation to reassure them that the car is everything they were looking for—they're making a good decision!

5. Use either/or questions in your closes. In the next chapter, we're going to give you twenty-five closes and objection-handling techniques, and they all include either/or questions. Use either/or to get them making decisions and to keep moving forward. It's closing on a minor point that leads to a major decision.

6. Be prepared to overcome their objections. Always have one more reason that they should get the car than the reasons they have to walk away.

7. Set yourself up for a win/win negotiation. Don't let price leak into the discussion until you know exactly what their objections are and how to build wins that overcome those objections.

REMEMBER: CLOSING IS A PROCESS

Most of us are told that any kind of commitment will do—just get them inside, get them on paper, and then we can figure it out. On the other hand, in a perfect world, we'd get 100 percent commitment from 100 percent of customers 100 percent of the time.

Reality is somewhere in between.

Today's buyer is either going to buy from you or they're going to leave, and chances are you'll never see them again. There are just too many options available to them. They aren't going to be patient with us forcing them into a negotiation, and we don't have the luxury of being so picky that we can prejudge people as "serious" or "committed" before we walk them through the sales process.

The sales process is the answer. If we disrupt their pattern from the very beginning, then we create an experience that they're more interested in entertaining. Those first steps—and bypassing early price and budget questions to keep the process intact—are vital, and they should happen for everyone, every time.

If we can't get a commitment even after trying, it's not a license to skip the close. If you tell your manager that it's time to start negotiating but the customer is still not on board, then you're still going to struggle to grind it out.

Involve your manager early and often to help you close the sale. Sometimes that higher authority sparks more commitment—as the customer, when the manager comes to talk to you, things feel serious and suddenly you can make a decision.

It helps to remember that you and your manager are on the same team. You're not the customer's advocate in a battle against the desk. You're working together with your manager to make that car fit into the customer's life and budget without taking a loss for the dealership. Use direct closing questions to get the commitment and hold it throughout the rest of the deal. Eliminate as many options as possible outside of getting the numbers right:

> *It sounds like you want to make sure you're getting a good deal, is that right? Other than us sitting down and you feeling comfortable with the deal and us fitting it in your budget, is there any other reason we couldn't wrap it up?*

If they still want to get the windows tinted and the custom wheels, ask again—*if we get that taken care of, is there any other reason we couldn't wrap it up?*

See the difference between direct questions and a weak, "What can I do to earn your business?" or "Let's see what we can work out"? We need to know exactly what we're dealing with and *close off all exits* before we start to negotiate the numbers. Corner the objections, make sure nothing else is hiding in there, and make sure they're committed on the car itself. There shouldn't be any surprises left about what they want or need.

And if you can't get a commitment, ask your manager—don't blow smoke about how it's time to start throwing numbers at the customer if there isn't a commitment on the table.

CUSTOMERS ARE GOING TO OBJECT.

IT'S THEIR JOB. OUR JOB IS TO OVERCOME THEIR OBJECTIONS

IF YOU THINK, YOU STINK—IT NEEDS TO BE INSTINCT

We're typically afraid of the objections that we'll get because we don't know how to respond to them. What do you say when someone tells you they're going to shop around, think about it, pray about it? How about when they say the price is too high, or try to get a price out of us before they'll commit?

Frictionless doesn't mean the customer never objects. You're rarely going to get lucky enough for that. Really, luck is just what happens when opportunity meets preparation. Closing questions aren't supposed to happen at a magical moment when they'll just say yes, pay full price, and end the deal. No—they are meant to flush out objections until there aren't any left. It's just a matter of preparation to be able to handle it.

In the rest of this section, we're going to walk through the things you can internalize and customize in order to make closing your instinct. It's going to take practice, and it's going to be uncomfortable. But if you can overcome your own objections to asking for the sale, you'll be able to overcome the customer's.

Time to face your fears. Let's go old-fashioned here—get out a pencil and paper and write them out. What's keeping you from asking for the sale? List everything. Then walk away for a little bit and come back to look at your list. Are those fears worth keeping you from the sale? Cross off anything unreasonable or unfounded, then make a plan to work on skills that will take care of the rest.

4 . 3

HOW TO CLOSE CONFIDENTLY

If you flipped right to this chapter of the book first, I recommend going back and starting at the beginning—but I completely understand. We all want those magic bullets that will make our jobs easier. But with endless closing scripts out there, I realized that a lot of people had a hard time understanding when to use each one of them and which ones are even worth using.

Closes are more than just scripts, and not all are created equal. Some work better as a first attempt, while others work well when you've been at it for a while. So, I've split them into three stages that you may or may not need in every instance, but that can help you sort out the closes into usable responses. Some of these closes can be used in multiple stages, but this will help you understand their context and applications.

At each stage, we're trying to eliminate anything that might keep the customer from committing to the car. In the past, we thought that meant coming to an agreement on price prior to negotiating. We might say something like "If I can sell you the car at a great price can we earn your business?" or "If I can make the terms and figures agreeable, would you drive it home right now?"

But who is making the commitment with that question? That's just me promising to drop the price. I'm negotiating with myself and the customer hasn't promised a thing.

The same goes for "Want to go see what we can do for you?" and "If we could give you a great deal..." Without defining what a great deal is, we're stepping into a negotiation blind, just hoping to grind something out that will make them ring the bell. Good closing questions draw those concerns and objections out so that you know exactly what you need to do to make that deal work for them.

If you've done your job but the customer still isn't feeling confident in the vehicle, you've earned the right to reassure them—having the right words and communicating them reflexively with conviction will transfer your confidence to the customer. Practice the closes that are in the next chapter so that they become conversational, instinctual responses—but also learn when and where they'll be useful to bring the customer closer to a commitment.

Not every deal will require closes from all three stages, because nothing will work 100 percent of the time. Our responsibility is to be prepared to capitalize on an objection with a close that will overcome it and move them toward a commitment—their commitment, not yours.

STAGE ONE: THE QUICK COMMITMENT

These come early in your closing phase. The Sold Row Close that I've referenced previously is one that I use almost every single time I take a customer out on the demo. This is stage one—just as the emotions from the second quadrant have peaked and the buyer is in love with the car—now it's time to close or lose.

As we're pulling back onto the lot and chatting about the drive, I'll say, "This car drove great, didn't it? Won't it be nice getting twenty-eight miles per gallon? Sounds like it's the perfect car for you guys. Go ahead and park it in the sold row and let's go inside to wrap it up so you can start enjoying it. Are you both going to be on the title or just one of you?"

When you've built up confidence and trust, this close works just about 100 percent of the time with 100 percent of the customers you take on a demo. Either they'll slow you down and start to give objections—which just gives you something to work off of—or they will park it and you'll be one step closer to making a deal.

Once you start getting commitments, firm them up with more actions and events. Say they tell you they both want to be on the title; keep them moving: "Hey, do me a favor. I've got bad eyes. Can you read me the miles for the odometer statement?"

Some things you might have them do to keep moving and firming up their commitment:

- Hang on to the keys so no one else drives your new car.
- Can you read me the last eight of the VIN?
- Put my business card on the dash so no one else drives it.
- Did you want to transfer plates or get new ones?
- Do you want a bottle of water or a cup of coffee?

The more actions, answers, and events they participate in, the more that decision is set in their mind. Even when objections come up, we can overcome them until we've eliminated all other options and they don't see any possibility other than taking that car home that day.

We've all heard that 80 percent of sales are closed after the fifth attempt. I don't know if that's true, but what I do know is that "you miss 100 percent of the shots you don't take."

STAGE TWO: DIG DEEPER

Objections are not a fault in the process—they're just a condition of the business and, once we're confident in our abilities to handle them, they're what we want. If we can't get a quick commitment, the next best option is to clarify, and corner the objections and overcome them. That's where stage two closes come in.

In stage two, we're climbing out of the car and don't have a commitment yet. They might be saying generic things like, "We never buy the first place we look." It's not an actual objection yet—you still need to dig deeper to get to the underlying concern.

> *I understand, but if you lost the keys to your house and found them in the first place you looked, would you keep looking? Of course not. Congratulations! I've found the keys to your new car right here. You both going to be on the title or just one of you?*

It sounds a little corny, but if we earn the right and say it confidently, it gets us past the reflexive hesitation and drives us toward an actual objection that can be overcome.

The workhorse for overcoming objections is a technique I call the Four Cs: Clarify, Change, Corner, and Close.

The initial closing questions are meant to draw out the objection. *Clarify* exactly what it is that's standing in the way between the customer and their commitment. When you finally draw it out—maybe they're worried about being able to afford the car and want to think it over, for example:

> *What is that you want to think about, the car itself or the price of the car?*

We then *change* the objection to budget because it is more flexible and easier to manage than price or payment.

> *It sounds like you're on a budget, is that right?*

Don't be afraid of these objections. We have many tools for the negotiation to help them justify stretching their budget (like the Gas Savings Close, Maintenance Close, or Total Cost of Ownership Close). Make sure you're on the same page, then *corner* that objection:

I understand you're on a budget, so other than us fitting this into your budget, is there any other reason we couldn't wrap this up?"

At that point, we can finally circle back to another closing question.

That's the easiest part of my job! Do you want a cup of coffee or a bottle of water while we go inside and finish this up?

Remember, something like "We're going to think about it" is not an objection. We have to dig deeper to clarify the actual objection if we want any hope of overcoming it. Otherwise, they'll just ask for your dismissal slip (that's your business card) and politely exit themselves to go to another dealership.

> Motion creates emotion. Keep them moving—reading, doing, following, choosing—and their emotions and engagement levels will stay high as well.

STAGE THREE: LAST-DITCH EFFORT

If the buyer walks off the lot, our chances of getting them back into the dealership are slim to none—and slim left town. Stage three closes are the final attempt when everything else has failed and we're about to see a buyer turn into a shopper.

This is when we need to have a little fun, make the interaction memorable, and still try to get that commitment if we can. It's the Hail Mary, and it's more about your interaction with them than anything else.

Communication is 7 percent words, 38 percent tone and inflection, and 55 percent body language. But if you don't have the right words to say, your body language is going to feel as lost as last year's Easter egg. If you haven't practiced the words, your tone and inflection will suck and will take away from whatever body language you might pull together.

YOU DON'T WANT TO BE THE NICEST SALESPERSON WHO *NEVER SOLD* THEM A CAR

If you get the right words (recognize), then practice them (internalize), then develop them into reflexive skills (customize), your interactions in stage three will come across how you want them to. You'll build the knowledge and skills and confidence into enthusiasm, and sales are made when you transfer your enthusiasm to the customer.

After we're sure that there are no other objections outside of budget or deal that we need to be aware of, we're set up and ready for the presentation of the first pencil. Now is when the fun starts—when we get to take all of the things we've learned about this person and put them into action just for them. If they're committed to buy and are starting to move from confidence into trust, a win/win negotiation is just around the corner.

There are plenty of tools to get you started in the next chapter of the book. If you're looking for more, I have some ready for you at frictionlessnegotiating.com. And if you're really wanting to step up your game, remember that I would love to come work side by side with you on the sales floor. But it doesn't matter who is with you or what materials you have, the difference-maker is you and how willing you are to practice. Put these in motion and see how often you can secure a commitment from your customers!

CHAPTER 5

TOOLS FOR FRICTIONLESS CLOSING

TIPS AND TECHNIQUES FOR CLOSING

Below are twenty-five closes and objection-handling techniques that will help you close more deals. The fact is that nothing will work all of the time, but to capitalize on their potential, they must be mastered. Whether or not you can secure the commitment right away, always stay positive and always have one more reason why they need to get the vehicle.

Before we get to the closes, here are a few keys to remember:

1. **Use Either/Or Closing Questions**. A good closing question isn't asking the customer if they want the vehicle or would they like to get it. A good closing question asks them how they want to own it. Always

remember to use an either/or closing question—not a yes/no—to get a commitment on the car.

2. **Lower the Customer's Defenses.** It's important to remember to start every close with a positive statement to lower their defenses, especially after you've asked for the sale and a customer objects. No matter how well you've executed the initial steps of the sale, closing and negotiation stages are the biggest pressure points of the deal.

3. **Set Up a Close.** Remember Feel-Felt-Found when you feel the customer has become defensive or guarded at the closing phase. Saying, "I understand how you feel" is a sign of listening and empathy; "I've felt the same way" lets them know you've been there before; and "What I've found was..." gives them a solution to their problem.

4. **The Power of Silence.** Overselling or talking too much is a closer's biggest enemy. Too often, salespeople get nervous during the closing and negotiation phases and tend to fill the silence with nervous chatter. Embrace the silence and talk to the deal, not through it.

> Nothing works 100 percent of the time. Remember the four SWs: Some will, some won't—so what? Someone is waiting. Next.

STAGE ONE CLOSES

THE SOLD ROW CLOSE

Situation: The Sold Row Close is used as you're pulling back onto the lot with the customer and now it's time to assume the sale and get a commitment on the car.

Application: The Sold Row Close is the first step of getting a commitment or flushing out an objection from the customer. This close should be executed properly 100 percent of the time with 100 percent of the customers that are taken on a demo. It consists of one or two feature-confirmation questions followed by a positive statement, then directing the action of parking in the Sold Row and wrapping it up with a closing question. This close will work almost 100 percent of the time because you will either get a commitment or flush out an objection.

Tips: Be confident. Be conversational. Have no fear.

THE ASSUMPTIVE CLOSE

Situation: The Assumptive Close is used in place of the Sold Row Close when the vehicle you're demoing is different from the one they're actually getting. This could be due to a special order, dealer trade, or something not currently available for sale.

Application: The Assumptive Close is the first step of getting a commitment or flushing out an objection from the customer. This close should be executed once the value has exceeded the price and it is short, sweet, and powerful. The key is to believe from the top of your head to the bottom of your toes that this is the perfect car for the customer. Start with a positive statement about how the car is exactly what they need, then finish with an either/or closing question to get a commitment on the car.

Tips: Be positive. Assume the sale. Trust the process.

THE REFLEX OBJECTION CLOSE

Situation: This close is typically used immediately after the Sold Row Close to get a commitment and keep the sale moving forward or to flush out an objection.

Application: The Reflex Objection Close is just a quick comeback after the customer's initial objection. You'll quickly find out whether it was a reflex response because they're nervous or if they have a true objection to buying. When the customer gives you that first objection after the Sold Row Close, just remind them that they deserve this vehicle, have worked hard for it, and it's perfect for them—then finish it with an either/or closing question. You'll find out really quickly if the objection was real or reflex.

Tips: Be conversational. Smile. Trust your execution.

THE CONFIRMATION CLOSE

Situation: You tried the Sold Row Close and/or Reflex Objection Close, but the customer still won't commit, and their objection is a generic one, like "We want to think about it."

Application: Closers know that when the customer objects, it may be real, but it can also be smoke. The Confirmation Close is most effective when you have a generic objection and you feel it's necessary to remind them everything they like about the vehicle. This close starts with two or three feature-confirmation questions, followed by a positive statement about the vehicle, and finishes with a closing question to get the commitment. It's effective at lowering the customer's defenses, reestablishing value, and putting them at ease.

Tips: Disarm. Relax. Be confident.

THE MAJOR BENEFIT CLOSE

Situation: The Major Benefit Close is a powerful close that is used when the customer gives a specific equipment or color objection.

Application: The power of the Major Benefit Close is that you are reducing the importance of a specific color or equipment objection and making a big deal out of the features that are most important to them. This can be used immediately after the Sold Row Close or later in the closing process, but is critical to use if you want to reduce the number of dealer trades you do. The great thing about this close is that it leverages their emotion while leading the decision to logic.

Tips: Be confident. Believe this is the perfect car. Sell the major benefits.

THE FOUR CS CLOSE

Situation: The Four Cs are used any time the customer's objection is vague, such as "We want to think about it," or is a specific price, trade, payment, deal, or discount objection.

Application: The Four Cs Close is the foundation for just about every Stage 2 and 3 Objection handling technique. This is a workhorse closing technique that, when perfected, can turn just about any objection into another opportunity to close. The power of the Four Cs is that it helps you to *clarify* their true objection, *change* it into something easier to handle, eliminate other potential objections by *cornering* it, followed by another *closing* question. Confidence is a closer's best friend and when you've mastered the Four Cs, you will feel ten feet tall and bulletproof.

Tips: Give choices. Embrace silence. Trust your practice.

STAGE TWO CLOSES

THE HESITATION CLOSE

Situation: The Hesitation Close is used when you feel controlling questions aren't the best method to overcome an objection with certain customers.

Application: The great thing about the Hesitation Close is that it empowers the customer and gives *them* the feeling of control. This close is an effective way to flush out an objection because it's as simple as making a positive response followed by an open-ended question to flush out what's holding them back. The key is to be quiet after the Open-Ended Question and let the customer tell you how to close them.

Tips: Be quiet. Listen to understand. Be prepared to transition into the Four Cs.

THE LOST KEY CLOSE

Situation: Use the Lost Key Close if, at any point, the customer's objection is "We never buy at the first place we look."

Application: The Lost Key Close is a fun way to break the ice and turn this potential shopper into a buyer. At this point of the sale you have nothing to lose, so have fun and go for it, and be prepared to execute the Four Cs once the customer gives you a real objection. Often, the initial instinct is that this is a corny or cheesy close—maybe it is—but use it and trust it, because it works. More times than not, the customer will laugh, then tell you what's truly holding them back, which then leads directly into changing the objection to budget using the Four Cs.

Tips: Have fun. Smile. Have positive body language.

THE BEN FRANKLIN CLOSE

Situation: The Ben Franklin Close is said to be a couple hundred years old, and unfortunately it's misunderstood and definitely underused. It's effective at two separate times in the sales process—early on when the customer won't land on a car and wants to leave, and after the demo when you've used multiple Stage One closes and still can't get a commitment on the car.

Application: Whether the customer's objection is early in the process or during the closing phase, the Ben Franklin Close is great for regaining control, using logic, getting the manager's involvement, and/or flushing out their real objection to buying. The pre-demo application is as simple as saying, "Before you leave, let's go inside and jot a few things down so you can take them with you to help you make a good decision." Then bring them inside and write out everything they want in their next vehicle and what they don't want in their next vehicle, followed by a manager intervening to help restart the deal. Use the same transition to the close post-demo, except list what they liked and didn't like to narrow down the real objection, then reclose. Worst-case scenario, the manager talks to the customer and they leave, but at least you know you did everything possible to close them.

Tips: Believe they're buying. Write everything down. People believe more of what they see than what they hear.

THE ROLE REVERSAL CLOSE

Situation: The Role Reversal Close is typically used after multiple Stage One closing attempts when you still get no results, and you just aren't sure what's holding them back.

Application: The simplest way to explain the Role Reversal Close is you are turning the tables on the customer and making them the salesperson. The result is that they end up telling you what it's going to take to sell them a car. Once they tell you their true objection, it's time to use the Four Cs to get a commitment so you can proceed to the negotiation.

Tips: Embrace the silence. Be sincere. Be empathetic.

THE INTERNET REPORT CLOSE

Situation: The Internet Report Close is used when you get a very specific objection based on the customer's price research. Typically, the objection is something like "We have an internet report that says we should be able to get this vehicle for $28,575; can you do that?"

Application: The key to the Internet Report Close is to embrace and compliment the customer on their research to lower their defenses. Start by conveying to them that you are happy they've done the research, tell them the benefits of their research, then change the objection to good deal, corner the objection to ensure there's nothing else that'll hold the deal up later, and reclose to get their commitment.

Tips: Start with a positive statement. Acknowledge their research. Persistence eliminates resistance.

TOTAL COST OF OWNERSHIP CLOSE

Situation: The Total Cost of Ownership Close will help you turn the "We can't afford higher payments than what we currently have" objection into another opportunity to close the customer.

Application: The foundation of the Total Cost of Ownership Close is to understand that what the customer's current payment is and what their actual monthly cost of ownership is are two different things. Once the customer gives you this objection, just make a positive statement to lower their guard. Ask them, "If I could show you how we could keep your monthly payments the same or potentially lower them, would you go ahead and get it?" The common response you'll get is "Absolutely," so now it's time to get to work on fitting the car into their budget.

Tips: Transfer your enthusiasm. Know their current fuel and repair expenses. Leverage logic.

THE AGREE AND CLOSE

Situation: The Agree and Close is a great way to lower a customer's defenses and reclose them when they just want to leave and shop around because they feel the car is just too much for them.

Application: The power of the Agree and Close is that your response is a pattern interruption. When the customer says that they think it might be too much car and they're not sure they can afford it, you just agree with them and tell them that's exactly why they need to get it. The typical customer response is "What do you mean?" At that point, just remind them that they told you the last vehicle they bought was less than they wanted and they weren't happy with it, and they don't want to make the same mistake this time.

Tips: Pattern interrupt. Reassure the choice. Be confident.

THE CHECK WITH MY SPOUSE CLOSE

Situation: The Check with My Spouse Close is pretty obvious when it needs to be used. Use anytime the customer says, "I need to check with my wife/husband/significant other before I get it."

Application: The first thing you need to do when you get this objection is to determine if it's real or just smoke. Great closers always assume the objection is smoke and they keep closing. The key to using this close is to lower their defenses, create a similar situation, get them to confirm and agree, then corner and reclose to get a commitment. Worst-case scenario, they leave—but at least you know you never gave up.

Tips: Always be closing. Assume it is smoke. No guts—no glory.

5 . 4

STAGE THREE CLOSES

THE SLEEP ON IT CLOSE

Situation: The customer's objection is pretty obvious, but the chances of getting them back if they leave are slim to none (and slim left town, remember?), so don't get weak now. This close is also effective with "We want to think on it overnight" and "We want to pray about it" objections from the customer.

Application: The Sleep On It Close is a great way to leverage the emotions you've created while leading the customer to a logical budget objection. You've earned the right to ask for the sale, so turn the customer's fear of buying into confidence and keep closing. The key is to make a positive statement, eliminate potential objections through a series of statements, validate that the vehicle is perfect for them, and reclose on the deal and/or budget.

Tips: Validate their decision. Know the Four Cs. Be confident.

THE TOO MUCH PRESSURE CLOSE

Situation: The Too Much Pressure Close is effective when the customer feels pressured or cornered into making a commitment. Everything is going great until you ask them to buy and they lose their mind.

Application: The most critical component of the Too Much Pressure Close is to apologize for your excitement and show remorse in your body language. The normal response from the customer is to apologize, then lower their defenses and tell you their real objection. (Time to reclose!) Let them know you understand what they're going through because most customers get nervous at this point and start feeling the pressure. Tell a story about how much you love helping customers by painting a picture of a similar situation with a customer and finish with a closing question to commit them or find out what's truly holding them back.

Tips: Body language sells. Control your tone and inflection. Keep closing.

THE FUTURE MARKET VALUE CLOSE

Situation: The Future Market Value Close is a great way to handle the objection "We just want to hold off to save for more money down and pay down our trade."

Application: The Future Market Value Close is powerful because it leverages logic and works best when a visual demonstration is used. The key is to get feedback from the customer when you explain that the cost of new vehicles typically goes up and the value of used cars goes down, which ultimately results in the customer putting themselves in a worse position. The conversation will naturally lead to a budget objection that sets you up to reclose and get a commitment.

Tips: Leverage logic. Write out the example. Trust your execution.

THE KITCHEN TABLE CLOSE

Situation: The Kitchen Table Close is best used when the customer's objection is a version of "We want to go home and talk about it."

Application: The Kitchen Table Close is effective because it leads the customer to visualize themselves talking later at home about what is holding them back from getting the car. The key is to lower their defenses with Feel-Felt-Found and paint a picture of a similar situation, followed by an open-ended question. This customer will pause, think, and tell you what's keeping them from making a decision now. If the objection is some form of money or deal, it's time to follow the Four Cs to commit the customer on the car.

Tips: Tell a story. Listen to understand. Embrace silence.

THE REPEAT METHOD CLOSE

Situation: The Repeat Method for closing is used to flush out and overcome virtually any objection at any time after your stage one attempts.

Application: The Repeat Method Close works because it causes a customer to clarify their intentions. This closing technique is simple to execute because it consists of repeating the last one or two words the customer says, looking at them like you're unclear of their meaning, and remaining quiet until they clarify their intentions. This process may take two or three times to flush out the true objection, and once they tell you what's actually holding them back, it's time to follow the Four Cs and get a commitment on the car now.

Tips: Silence is strength. Body language sells. Sell it hard.

THE TIME IS MONEY CLOSE

Situation: The Time Is Money Close works best with a customer who is a professional that understands the value of their time. Their objection will be a version of "We want to shop around and see if we can save some money."

Application: The Time Is Money Close is all about creating doubt, using logic to explain that we all pay about the same for cars, and convincing them that their time is worth more than the potential savings they might get. When this close is properly used, the customer's response is typically some form of price, deal, or budget, which gives you the perfect opportunity to corner and reclose to get a commitment on the car.

Tips: Create doubt. Leverage the value of their time. Be confident.

THE LONG-TERM SAVINGS CLOSE

Situation: The Long-Term Savings Close is most commonly used when the customer's objection is "I think this may be too much car" and "We're going to shop around and see if we can find something a little less expensive."

Application: The Long-Term Savings Close is effective because it combines the emotions of getting the right vehicle with the logic of past decisions. Always start with disarming their objection using Feel-Felt-Found, then reassure them that you can help them get less car if that's the direction they choose, address their pain points from the past, and reclose by leveraging the emotion you've created earlier in the sales process.

Tips: Disarm the objection. Reassure the customer. Leverage logic.

THE HOME DELIVERY CLOSE

Application: The Home Delivery Close is for that customer who tells you that they definitely want the car but don't have time today and will be back later in the week.

Situation: The Home Delivery Close is perfect to handle the customer who says they want the car and will be back, but you're not buying it. We all know what a customer says isn't always what they mean, so let's find out if it's true or just an excuse to escape. Always start this close with a positive statement to lower their defenses, eliminate their objection by explaining to them that you'll deliver the car and paperwork to their house or work, and close on the day/time to deliver the car. They'll either pick a day/time (and that's a great thing!) or you'll find out if it was an excuse to escape (and then they'll usually come clean about what's actually holding them back).

Tips: Don't give up. Be different. *Always Be Closing*.

THE BULLY CUSTOMER CLOSE

Situation: The Bully Customer Close is for that extremely tough customer that will not let you follow the sales process and adamantly demands your best price—to the point of being rude.

Application: The best way to handle a bully is to confront them directly. The Bully Customer Close works because it's a pattern interruption from what they're expecting. After you've tried everything to redirect them to the sales process and they're still in your face, just look at them confidently and say, "I've been waiting for a customer like you all day long. Someone that knows exactly what they want. Whip out your checkbook, follow me, and we'll get you out of here in your new car as soon as possible," then turn around and start walking inside. There are three potential outcomes: 1) They leave without buying. 2) They say something like, "We haven't even driven it yet," which allows you to get the sale back on track. Or 3) They follow you inside, where you get your manager involved and sell them a car. The bottom line is if you sell them, they'll usually end up being one of your best customers.

Tips: No fear. Be confident. Remember the four SWs.

THE WHOLE WORLD CLOSE

Application: The Whole World Close is a fun, last-resort close when every other close has failed to commit the customer and they are about to leave.

Situation: The Whole World Close isn't for everyone, but if you like to have fun, have the ability to tell a story, enjoy laughing with your customers, and have no fear of closing—this is for you. The power of the Whole World Close is that it draws the customer into a story about you being a child and your grandparents' house, then ends with a fun closing question. The worst thing that can happen is the customer still leaves without buying, but they will remember you above all other salespeople.

Tips: Paint a picture. Laugh. Have fun.

THE CHEESEBURGER CLOSE

Situation: The Cheeseburger Close is an amusing, last-resort close for the customer that says, "We definitely want the car, but we're going to grab a bite to eat first and then we'll be back."

Application: I understand that most salespeople are afraid of using the Cheeseburger Close because it's a little corny—but understanding the purpose and application is important. The thought process behind it is to determine whether the objection is real or if it's smoke. It could be either, but my job is to find out. So when they say, "We definitely want the car but we're going to grab a bite to eat first and then we'll be back," just say, "That's great, I've been busy all day and haven't had a chance to eat. Could you grab me a burger or something when you come back?" Then hand them a $20, watch their body language, and wait for their response. It'll typically be "No Problem" or they'll pause, look at each other, and then tell you what's really holding them back. If they say they'll grab you some food, that's a good thing. If they give you a specific objection, just follow the Four Cs and turn the shopper into a buyer.

Tips: Observe their body language. Control your tone and inflection. Relax and have fun.

PART III

FRICTIONLESS NEGOTIATING

CHAPTER 6

NEGOTIATE FOR GROSS

RE-IMAGINING
NEGOTIATION

It's time for the elephant in the room—or maybe not quite the elephant, since everyone wants to talk about it. It's the challenge to our current thinking and processes that we don't like. By this point, I'm sure that some of you reading this want to get in a fistfight with me or pile on me on the internet, calling me an idiot.

I get it. This is tricky stuff, and I don't expect that all of you will be able to do all of the things I'm talking about here. All I expect is for you to have an open mind.

While I know how much success waits on the other side of this process, I also know it's a lot of work. Most people aren't willing to put in the effort and practice that it takes to become a great negotiator. Instead, we make excuses that justify why our techniques (or lack of them) don't work:

They all have a TrueCar report...

They're more informed than they use to be...

They don't want to be pressured...

Customers don't want to negotiate...

Whatever we try to use as a reason not to negotiate will just be an excuse that holds us back. Think about what happened when you bought something that you thought would take some negotiation, but the seller agreed with the first price. That doesn't feel like a win, does it? It just makes you wonder whether you could have gotten a better deal. That's because we all want to feel like we earn our wins.

We all *want* to negotiate. Let's re-imagine how that might look.

When you sit down to a bacon-and-eggs breakfast, who made a bigger commitment—the chicken or the pig? The chicken just donated, but the pig's all in. If you want to make a difference in your success as a salesperson, be the pig. Go all in on the process and don't look back.

NEGOTIATION WORKS IF YOU WORK IT

I started this book with the historical perspective of the industry and today's buyer perspective because they eliminate our excuses. When we know what's going through the customer's mind when they come onto the lot, and we understand why our existing processes are outdated, it's not as easy to tell ourselves those limiting stories anymore.

At the end of the day, we're only grinding out deals because we've gotten too afraid to close and don't know how to set up and execute a deal that works for everyone. They're coming in with an internet report because they want a good deal and it allows them to start the negotiation, and whoever starts the negotiation wins. So, when salespeople complain about customers not being the same as they used to be and how they don't want to negotiate, we're just telling ourselves stories.

It's not negotiating that's the problem. It's us. Customers aren't trying to avoid negotiating—they're just better at it than we are. They're coming in with information and details that can help them start the numbers conversation, while we plug away with our old processes, wondering why it's not working.

There's no magic dust to sprinkle over your negotiation table that will make it work every time. But if you take everything that we've learned about the buyer and the process, and combine it with these techniques, you'll get a heck of a lot closer than you will trying to just grind it out.

Bottom line: negotiating works. If you understand it, if you follow the rules and develop the skills, negotiation can make a customer experience better, make more deals work, *and* bring in more gross.

BAD HABITS OF NEGOTIATING

1. Being afraid to negotiate. Maybe you don't have the skills yet, or you don't know how to overcome objections. Maybe you're more afraid of losing the deal than you are inspired to make it. This is the first bad habit and it affects almost all of us at one time or another.

2. Not having a commitment. If you never lowered the customer's guard, never created mental ownership, and didn't get a commitment from the customer, negotiation becomes difficult or impossible. Working out the numbers without getting a commitment happens sometimes, but it should be the exception, not the rule.

3. Taking too long. Time is our customers' number one commodity. Showing up disorganized, unprepared, and taking forever will kill the experience and maybe even the deal.

4. Relying on the worksheet. It's nice to have a good worksheet that looks pretty, but a bunch of numbers on a paper or a tablet isn't negotiating. It's offer-presenting.

5. Working the manager harder than the customer. You're not the buyer's agent—you don't represent them to the manager. Remember: sympathy is hopping down into the hole with someone who's stuck and trying to make them feel better while they're down there; empathy is getting a ladder to help them out of the hole.

BAD HABITS IN GOOD TIMES

Before the recession and before the internet, we were pretty good at negotiating, as an industry. Because the customer didn't have much information beyond basic pricing, limited trade value info, and almost no access to payment calculators, we had the advantage to create options for them that they would be happy with. But that stretch of time—starting around 2008—posed some of the oddest challenges for us in the history of selling cars. Customer confidence was down, they were price-shopping heavily and calculating payments before they came in the door, and we were just grateful to see anyone at all. When people came in to buy a car, the last thing we wanted to do was negotiate.

That's when desperation set in and we just wanted to make a sale as easy as possible. We weren't selling cars anymore—people were coming in and buying them. The most we would do was present multiple payment and down payment options, hoping the customer would pick one. They were on our lot. They knew what they wanted. And we didn't want to scare them away.

When we go into the negotiation scared that we're going to lose the deal and desperate to make it, it's like playing prevent defense in football. You're playing not to lose instead of playing to win and, more times than not, the only thing it *prevents* is you winning.

Even though the economy has bounced back and we've sold more cars year after year consistently for a decade now, we've hung on to these bad habits. We still feel so desperate to make a sale that we become passive. People are coming onto the lot inspired to buy a car, and we don't know how to sell to them anymore.

I've been in car sales both before the recession and after, and I can tell you that there were challenges on either side. Universally, we've always had to build value. We've always had to get the customers excited. We've always needed committed buyers, and we've always had to leverage that commitment, excitement, and value to create a good deal in negotiations.

In fact, the excuse that the internet eliminated negotiations or that customers are too informed is so far off that the opposite is true. Maybe in the old days the customer didn't have many other places to go if they had a bad experience, but today we have a lot more challenges to overcome to create a great experience. Some of these cars only have about $200 worth of profit built into the MSRP—so it's made our job of negotiating a win/win and holding gross even tougher.

They might come in with payments already calculated and a price range they should pay, but if we follow the sales process, we can work out other options to build value and remove objections, like Prepaid Maintenance and Total Cost of Ownership Closes. There's no reason to grind out a deal when we can work *with* the customer instead of working *on* them.

The catch is that we have to get creative to make these things work. Printing out a worksheet is not negotiating. Your words, your tone, your inflection, your confidence, and the victories you build in for the customer are.

Do we really know how to sell cars? Can we negotiate for maximum down payment? Do we know how to negotiate for maximum payment? Do we know how to justify their trade value? Can we adapt when times get tough again, or are we going to become extinct?

The rest of this section can start to shape your answers.

> Bad habits are formed during good times, and for ten years, we've created a whole lot of bad habits that won't sustain us through the next pullback.

GROSS DOESN'T KILL VOLUME

A common misconception in our industry is that a win/win outcome isn't possible. We've become so worried about not losing deals that we don't even try to negotiate for gross—or if we do try to make money, we decide that it will probably come at the expense of volume. I remember having this conversation with one of the dealers that was interested in working with me. The owner told me from the beginning, "I don't want you coming in here and putting in a system that will hold more gross profit at the expense of our volume and market share."

His concern is one that lots of dealers have. They're worried that holding gross will cut into volume. So often, we wind up chasing volume bonuses from the factory so hard that we lose $100,000 to try to make $150,000. It's creating a race to the bottom that will break the car industry completely if we let it.

VOLUME IS YOUR JOB— GROSS DETERMINES HOW WELL YOU DO IT

I don't believe consumers really want that race to the bottom anyway. One study said that 79 percent of car shoppers are looking for value and quality at a fair price, while only 21 percent are focused on price alone.[3] Amazon isn't winning because of their prices—they're winning because of convenience. We have to make our negotiation processes convenient, quick, and efficient. We need to set up built-in victories for customers.

Just like that dealership, we have to challenge the way that we think about the negotiation and the goal of our sales process. I told him, "Look, if you do what I show you, if you follow the process 100 percent, this is going to work. You don't have to lose volume or gross. Just trust the process."

The management team decided to become 100 percent committed to the process, and they went from selling cars at a loss on the majority of their deals to loser deals being the exception. This was due to a massive culture change in their beliefs, processes, and expectations and, at the time I'm writing this book, their profits are up by seven figures year over year—and just as importantly, their market share has also increased at the same time.

3   Max Digital and Erickson Research, "The 2017 Dealer Trust & Transparency Survey," https://maxdigital.com/whitepapers/dox/MAXDigital_Trust_ResearchReport_f.pdf.

All right, fess up: which of those bad habits of negotiating have you done this year? This month? Have you done any of them today? It's okay to admit it. Habits are things that we do without thinking about them. Our goal in this book and anytime I train someone is to put better habits in their place. Pick one and decide you're going to work to eliminate it, then keep reading to see what you can do instead.

GOLDEN RULES OF NEGOTIATION

Over the years, as I would teach classes and speak at conferences, I'd often tell the group, "The number one rule of negotiation is..." By the end of the event there would be five or six *number one* rules.

Eventually, I stopped trying to find that magic button and admitted that there are a set of rules that good negotiations follow. Like the Golden Rule, they keep the other person centered. These rules are for both volume and holding gross, while at the same time understanding that every customer is different.

Don't forget that you are part of the win/win equation as well. If you're not going to work on your own wins, you might as well give the customer your ATM card and

PIN and let them take money directly out of your bank account.

RULE 1: NEGOTIATING IS OPTIONAL

Sticker's quicker, as the old saying goes. If you go into every sale thinking that you *have* to negotiate, you'll never hold maximum gross profit. While a lot of your deals will turn into second- and third-pencil negotiations, it doesn't mean every one has to.

There are a lot of things that we buy without negotiating. Why can't cars be the same?

When we approach the end of a deal so excited for the customer and the value that we've built for them, it changes our mindset. We're thinking about how much we've connected with them and how much they love their car, and asking for sticker price feels like a steal compared to what the car means to them.

No one hopes they miss the putt once before sinking it, or hopes they brick the free throw. If you do, you'll definitely miss. So don't hope or expect that the deal will take multiple pencils. Hope for sticker. Hope that they agree to the first pencil and the negotiation won't be necessary.

You might only ever find a couple of people who will pay

sticker, but that doesn't matter. Believe that you have a great product, that it's fairly priced, and that you can show people how they can't afford to pass it up. The value far exceeds the price, so there's no reason to believe negotiating will be necessary.

RULE 2: NEGOTIATE OUT OF INSPIRATION, NOT DESPERATION

Stop being afraid to negotiate. Turn that fear into fun. JFK said it this way: "Let us never negotiate out of fear, but never fear to negotiate."

Negotiating is about knowing what you want, going after it, and respecting the customer in the process. The whole point is to get to a win/win outcome, which means you need to look out for yourself while being willing to give a little in order to satisfy both parties. It's building a relationship rather than burning bridges.

When you have kept the customer top of mind through the whole process, by now they're starting to trust you. This is where it can all pay off, not just for them but for you as well. If you've helped them see themselves in that vehicle, now it's time to help fit it into their budget. With all of your closes and tools ready and internalized, you're able to ease their mind and find solutions for whatever problem brought them to the lot that day.

RULE 3: WHOEVER CARES LEAST ABOUT A DEAL WINS

Technically, this is "whoever *appears to* care least." The customer needs to want to get the car more than it seems like we want to sell it. The customer needs to want that car so badly that they'll do whatever it takes to make that happen—that emotion is what will make them more flexible throughout the negotiation.

For the first three quadrants, we've found out about their wants, needs, compelling reasons, challenges, and desires, then given them a solution for each of those concerns in the perfect vehicle for them. We've painted that vehicle into their life so well that they can't imagine any other vehicle helping them more than this one. We've got them licking the paint off the car, so to speak...and none of it should appear to matter to us personally.

A Beggar's Close attempt looks like desperation and takes the attention off of the buyer and onto what you need. It eliminates trust and sends the customer all the way back to being guarded.

Instead, we should convey so much confidence in the deal with our tone and body language that it looks like we're willing to get up and walk away. We're not begging. We're negotiating. There should absolutely be a difference.

RULE 4: WHOEVER STARTS THE NEGOTIATION HAS THE ADVANTAGE

Anytime we start talking numbers, the negotiation has begun. When we find out how much they're "looking to spend," what their credit looks like, what kind of down they have, what they owe—all of that is related to the negotiation. Usually, because our sales process made that the focus and we've conditioned the customers to bring these things up early on.

In these cases, either they're starting the negotiation and will have the advantage, or we're initiating the price conversation way too early and will give our advantage away.

As the old saying goes, the biggest bump you'll ever get is the one you never hear. If we ask the customer where they want to be and find out it'll be $300 a month with zero down, the first pencil being $6,700 down and $876 a month will look like a Grand Canyon–sized gap. But if we never find out those numbers at all, then the first pencil will pull out their top numbers instead of the unrealistic numbers we often get. They focus on their worst-case payment scenario and throw out their top numbers like $2,500 and $475 a month.

Thinking about houses again, you'd never hear a real estate agent ask you, "Well, the listing price is $289,000— how close to that are we going to get? Keep in mind what it cost to build..." Of course we want a steal of a deal. Of course we don't want to pay as much as it's worth. It doesn't matter. What we want to offer on the house is determined by the listing prices and that gets our thinking up, gets the conversation started, and keeps the negotiation reasonable.

Meanwhile, in the car industry we've spent sixty years letting the customer start the negotiation. It's time to change that.

By being the first person to throw out numbers, we cover a ton of ground from the very beginning without having to pull them there. That $2,500 and extra $175 will be the biggest bump of the negotiation, and we'll only get it if we're the ones to start the negotiation.

RULE 5: BUILD IN REMOVABLE OBJECTIONS

This step is simple but effective: put things into the negotiation that you can afford to take out. From the very first pencil, give yourself plenty of room to adapt. For example, that $6,700 down at forty-eight months is not there to get the customer real or peel them off the ceiling. Those are all removable objections that will shape the rest of the negotiation.

When we drop from $6,700 to $5,000, then finally settle

on $2,500, how does the customer feel about that transaction? They feel like they've won. For some of them, getting multiple wins matters even more than the size of the wins themselves. It's the victory that makes the difference.

If the first pencil starts at seventy-two or eighty-four months with zero down, there's no room to win. There are no removable objections other than price and trade value, and that causes the gross to suffer in the long run.

Think about it this way: if you were to go into a casino and the house offered you $50,000 to gamble with, would you use that or your own cash? It's the same thing here. As salespeople, we should be negotiating with the customer's money. Pull the concessions from the down and payments, but hang on to the price and trade as long as possible. Every time you discount the car or give more for the trade, you're giving your own money away. Every time you focus on budget, it's the customer's money, and they showed up ready to spend it.

Remember that each of these rules, tools, and quadrants are meant to create a repeatable process. Follow the steps over and over, regardless of the outcome. Football coaches don't motivate their players in their pregame speech by saying, "We're going to win 28-14 today; now get out there and kick their ass!" That wouldn't do a thing.

Instead, they make sure the first seven plays are scripted out, remind everyone to do their job on each play, and execute every step as planned. When that happens, the touchdowns take care of themselves.

Follow the Golden Rules. Stick to the process. Internalize and customize the scripts. Keep the buyer at the center of the deal, and the wins will take care of themselves.

> The heart of the Golden Rules is keeping the customer in mind the whole time. Sometimes we struggle to remember to consider gross too. We can have both! That's the goal of a win/win, after all. Think back over the last time you negotiated with a customer. Were you more of a buyer's agent or an offer presenter? How can you hold for gross longer, or deliver for your customers better? Keep reading!

HOW TO NEGOTIATE WITH YOUR CUSTOMER INSTEAD OF YOURSELF

We only have about thirty minutes to wrap up the deal after the demo where the customer is still excited and running off of that emotional high. You can see it start to wear off—so clearly, in fact, that we use to call it being "under the ether."

Think about going in for surgery. The anesthesiologist gives you the speech about how you're going to go under and be out like a light and then before you know it they'll start waking you up.

"For thirty minutes, you won't see or feel anything at all."

Now imagine that they put the shot in your arm, and you

start to fade. Before you go all the way out, the doctor comes in and says, "All right, the surgery will be about an hour. See you then!"

Pump the brakes, man! I want out!

The same thing happens in the negotiation. Once you hit that thirty-minute mark, the ether starts to wear off and they begin to get uncomfortable. They're antsy, they're looking around, losing interest, getting impatient, and getting buyer's remorse before they even buy...and why wouldn't they? If we're disappearing for fifteen minutes at a time, going back and forth over and over again to the manager, or churning through things we should have already completed and talked about, we look like amateurs. We're the hospital staff who couldn't communicate.

They want to negotiate with us—they just don't want to negotiate with amateurs. No amount of emotion that was built from even the best presentation can overcome that kind of logical (or illogical) pain.

We've all heard the theory that the happiest customer is typically the one we make the most money on. Why is that? I think it's because we work harder to give those customers a good experience. When we do a better job with them from start to finish, their satisfaction isn't just about what they paid. It's about the overall experience.

Fully engaging our customers from the Pre-demo Trade Walk to the last pencil and signature on the dotted line makes that experience work. Anything less than that is just a negotiation with ourselves.

THE FOUR OUTCOMES OF NEGOTIATION

Lose/lose. If we get to the end of the negotiation and the customer doesn't get the car, we both lose. Even worse, they typically don't feel very good about their experience and we don't feel good about the customer. They're not likely to ever come back. Their negative perceptions around car sales continue, and we keep telling ourselves stories. We take it personally, grumble about wasting three hours of our time, and use it as an excuse the next time around to take shortcuts. Sometimes lose/lose will happen even with a better process in place—we can only do our best, after all. The trick is to keep our mindset in the right place for the next time.

Win/lose. We've sold the car. We've even made some money on it, and we're happy with the huge commission we're going to get from it. But how does the customer feel? If it was a bad experience, they've lost, even if the car is perfect for them. Maybe we didn't connect with them or didn't do a good job building value. Maybe we didn't set the negotiation up the right way. Sometimes they don't realize they're in a bad situation until later. If we let them go right to zero down, eighty-four months, then they've got $6,000 of negative equity and no flexibility to trade up and out when the time comes. A win/lose is when they got the vehicle because they needed it, but the experience was less than exceptional. The real problem here is that we'll only ever get that one win from that customer—they won't be back for more.

> I'm not saying that you'll never do an extended loan with zero down. It happens. But it needs to happen as a last resort. We need to do everything in our power to show them the right way to get their vehicle and make them earn it with their eyes open to the drawbacks. We're in the people business, not the car business—the relationship comes first.

Lose/win. This is the customer that grinds our teeth off. We lose money on the car just to get an RDR and to have something burning gas and busting bugs. They might have gotten the car they wanted at the price they wanted, but we only sold it out of desperation. Like the win/lose, this kind of deal doesn't often create loyalty. It's not good in the short term or the long term, even if the customer seems happy about it. Sometimes they think they've won by getting a screaming deal—but rarely do they feel good about it, no matter how great it was. Plus we lost money, and the last time I checked, that's not the goal of being in business. Ultimately, no one will feel good about the deal.

Win/win. If we do it right, a win/win negotiation is really a win/win relationship that we're creating. A win for the customer is when they feel like they got a good deal. They got the vehicle that they love from a salesperson who will take care of them long-term, and it all fit within their budget.

On our side, we win when we've followed the process and showed them the best way to get their new vehicle. When we finally closed the deal, the customer was in the shortest term possible, fitting it into their budget as equitably as possible, and we made money on the deal. There's no such thing as a win where we've lost money, and there's no win if the customer didn't have a good experience that also created a long-term benefit.

If we set our sights on a win/win and follow the right process to get there, no matter what deal we come to, we can know that we did our absolute best for the customer and our careers.

HOW NEGOTIATING PLAYS OUT

At the point of negotiation, the customer's emotions won't get any higher. The demo has made it peak, and now they're starting to come down toward logic the more time we take to wrap up the deal. If conversations about price and budget happened instead of value, their emotion levels won't be high at all, and we won't ever be able to get it back.

What's worse, if we half-heartedly negotiated on the lot about their budget and ideal payment, when we sit down to run the actual numbers, it's going to be painful. The customer will have no emotional attachment to the car, they will have started the deal, and we will be stuck having to drop the price down to meet their numbers. The further apart we are, the louder the customer's logic is going to get, and we will be perceived as having no credibility—just a stereotypical car salesperson. They'll drop back to guarded, and we will have lost any trust that we had earned.

None of this is an exaggeration. Talking price too early will absolutely kill your deals.

For all of the effort we put into bypassing numbers and holding the process intact, we also have to know how to present the numbers once it's time. From the first time we present the first set of numbers (the first pencil) to wrapping up the deal, we need to be confident, stay focused, and control emotion levels—both ours and the customer's.

Ideally, this is the first time that numbers should be discussed with the customer. Remember, it's not just the worksheet that matters here. Words, tone and inflection, body language, and the presentation are absolutely key. If we come out swinging with a worksheet full of surprises—less for their trade than they expected, retail price, 20 percent down at forty-eight months—without having the necessary skills, it will turn into an atomic pencil. The customer will go ballistic—will we ever be able to lower their blood pressure again? But if the same numbers are presented with skill and confidence, everything about the negotiation changes:

> *Great news, the car's still available; let me show you the best way to get it. For our car, with your trade, and the fees. By the way, we'll pay your car off in full, and with your initial investment of $6,700, it puts your monthly investments at $876. Give me your okay right here, and we'll wrap it up.*

That's not making assumptions or making them feel cornered with a bunch of shocking numbers. It's showing them the best way, even if it ends up not being their way. If they shut it down, we're not offended or hung up on anything:

Customer: We don't have that kind of money to put down.

No big deal, it's not a requirement—it's just a better deal for you. The more you put down, the less you finance, the more you save in interest, and the more flexibility you'll have so you can trade out of it when you want to instead of when the bank says you can. Keeping that in mind, how close to $6,700 were you thinking? More like $5,000?

Now, when they respond with—*heck no, maybe $2,500?*—we just got closer to their top numbers that they think they can afford instead of the lowest numbers they hoped they could get away with. Now we get to negotiate from their top numbers up instead of grinding them up from unrealistic numbers if we had let them start the negotiation.

NEVER ASK THEM WHAT THEY WANT TO SPEND– *ALWAYS* GIVE A NUMBER

My goal is to always try to refocus and redirect the conversation. When the first pencil is structured properly, the biggest factor on the table is usually down payment and payment, so we should try to refocus every price, payment, or trade conversation to down payment.

Keep in mind that slow kills at this point more than ever—our goal is to have it done in thirty minutes, before the ether wears off. Make it quick. You shouldn't be away from your customer for more than five minutes at a time, since leaving them alone is one of the worst things you can do. Get back in there, don't tell stories, don't make small talk with your managers, and wrap up the deal.

Not only does speed come from our own efficiency, but we can transfer that urgency onto the buyers:

> *Hey, I'm going to go double-check and make sure that car's still available. I'm sure it is. I just want to make sure there aren't any other deposits or pending deals on it. We've got twelve sales-people here and sometimes that happens. We should be good, but I want to be sure.*

When the customer feels that urgency, it plants the seed that they need to make a decision, or they might lose that deal forever. Then we get to relieve that pressure by starting on a positive:

Great news! That car is available. There are no deposits on it or anything, so let me show you the best way to get it.

An uneven split can sometimes create an even split: *How close to $50,000 were you thinking, maybe $49,500?* By only offering a small gap as a suggestion, they have to come up higher to give the feel of that split. Say they come back with $47,000; we can do it again: *I'm not sure if we can. Other than getting my manager to split the difference at oh, say, $48,900, is there any other reason...?* They'll probably ask for a fair split at $48,250, and we can plant doubt again: *I'm not sure about that, but other than getting my manager to do, I don't know, $48,500...?* Once you get a confirmation, clean it up by refocusing on down and payment in the same way. Use specific numbers, and get them as close as possible before you move on from that pencil.

When you present the numbers, don't fall back on the standard, "So what do you guys think?" Instead, go back to a close. Recommit them to the deal before you move on to the next step:

Let me see if I have this right. Other than getting this to you for $2,200 down and getting your monthly investment to $479 a month, is there any other reason we couldn't wrap it up?

Corner the objection and get them to recommit to their numbers. The best way to start the second pencil is to finish the first pencil the right way. You don't have to commit to those numbers—*I'm not sure we can do these numbers, but I'm going to go work for you* creates doubt and a fear of loss that turns into urgency for the buyer, all while you're reassuring them that you're going to do everything possible to make it work.

Don't forget that sometimes you'll have to negotiate on price and not just down and payment, at least for some customers. Some will come in paying cash, but the majority will be focusing on financing or leasing. It doesn't do any good to negotiate on a price if down and payment is the main hot button. At the same time, when you reach an agreement on price with the price-focused customer, clean up the down and payment before you take the deal back to your manager. Then tell them that you've never seen a price that low and you're going to go to work for them.

> Goal: Get all you can and take what you can get.
>
> Remember: We're showing them the best way to get their new vehicle, then lowering their anxiety if it isn't going to work for them. This isn't personal. It's logical, and it's up to us to keep the emotions focused on budget instead of price. Eighty percent of your negotiation is determined by how effective you are on the first pencil, and the best way to start it is to set it up right from the very beginning. It's not about them signing off on the first set of numbers, it's about you working to pull out their top numbers and setting up the second pencil the right way.

SECOND PENCIL

For too long, we've had a fundamental flaw in how we negotiate. We spend all of our time trying to get a customer to understand and make our payment, and ignore the fact that they brought their current payment with them. We focus on getting them to agree on our $600 per month when they already spend $475 per month. The reality is that we only need to help them find and justify making an additional $125 per month, and that's what the second pencil is all about.

If you did your job on the first pencil and pulled out their top numbers, it's time to use the information you gathered during the Pre-demo Trade Walk to close this deal. This is the perfect time to use things like the Gas Savings Close to show them what their total monthly expense is. Sure, they may only be paying $475 to the bank, but what are the additional expenses they have now that they won't have on the new vehicle—like gas savings and repairs? Focus your energy on finding their total monthly cost of ownership to leverage logic and close the sale.

Throughout the deal, we've been gathering information that will help us be effective at closing the deal. If we make it through the first pencil and don't have a deal yet (which is usually the case), we can now use that information along with their top numbers to effectively fit the vehicle into their budget. You got all you could and took what you could get on the first pencil; now is the time to get creative, justify your numbers, and help them see how they can afford this vehicle. This is where we get to give our customers choices.

This one isn't as cookie-cutter as the "best option" first pencil. We might do an A/B pencil where one gives them the payment they want with an extended term and more money down, while B gives them the down they want with a little higher payment:

> *Good news, guys! I think I'm pretty close to where you want to be. Now, we do need a little help. If payment's most important, we need a little help on down, and if down payment is most important, we need a little help on the payment. Which one works best for you?*

Just like we did when we closed on the sale, once we get an answer, we assume the sale.

> *Great. Are you going to put that down on your credit card or are you going to write a check for it?*

Every time we're presenting numbers, whether it's the first, second, or last pencil, assume they're going to agree. Let them object, of course, but don't carry any preconceived notions of what the objection will be. If they speak up and say they can't afford the down, that's fine—close them on the higher payment option and assume the sale.

If neither payment works, we can really get creative. Look at the gap between where you are and where they want to be—where can that amount be made up in their budget? This draws the focus to the smaller number rather than the total payment. Maybe that amount will be covered in gas savings or in what they're currently spending on repairs and maintenance.

> *Remember earlier you were telling me that you drive about seventy-five miles a day, right? And your current car gets fifteen miles a gallon and your new one's going to get twenty-five miles a gallon. So, if you just do basic math on that, you're using five gallons of gas per day on your current car, and three gallons of gas on your new car. That means you're saving two gallons of gas a day at thirty days.*

> *Sixty gallons per month at $3 a gallon means you're saving $180 per month in real cash that's going into your pocket versus into your gas tank. It looks like we found your $73, with $107 left over. Do you want your first payment in thirty days or forty-five days?*

Another approach might be to give them an A/B/C pencil, with the last option being a lease. They're going to like that option the most, and we can explain it to them.

Sometimes they'll object and say they don't lease, but your response is to say, "That's a shame..." and explain the benefits of a lease; now they have another option that they hadn't necessarily considered before.

If you haven't practiced or prepared, you'll fall right back into being an offer presenter instead of a professional negotiator. Customers don't have patience for amateurs who are just running back and forth to their manager's office.

Lean on the logic of negotiation here and explain what you're asking and why. Justify the trade value and how you arrived at that number. Justify the down payment and why it's beneficial. The fear of losing a deal is important, but being able to justify your numbers is critical.

> Goal: Get creative to help fit the vehicle into the customer's budget.
>
> Remember: Think about total cost of ownership, not just the expense of the vehicle. Everything you learned earlier in the deal will feed into what you know about the customer here. Show them what they're spending and how this car reduces that spend or their pain points to help them justify the expense in favor of the value.

THIRD PENCIL

If you get to the third pencil, it's time to just sell the car and wrap up the deal or walk the customer. Hopefully, we won't make it to this point very often. For the times that we do, I suggest that you only go out if it's just to congratulate the customer and use the Shake and Bump Close to ensure no money is left on the table. If there still needs to be some negotiating, I believe this pencil needs to be presented by a manager or someone of higher authority that can make a decision to negotiate on the spot or walk the customer.

We've already gotten creative with the second pencil and found additional money in the customer's budget. Now we want to get one last bump out of them and then shake hands. Assuming we did a great job on the second pencil and got the customer's commitment, it's time to go for the last bump and make sure we're not leaving any money on the table:

Hey, my manager wanted me to ask if you're going to let $7.42 per month keep you from getting a new car today?

Whether they say no or an emphatic *hell yes*, the answer is the same:

Congratulations, that's exactly what I told him.

Either way, it's a win for you and the customer. If they say *Hell yes*, you know you got all you could and the customer feels like you went to bat for them. If they say *No,* you won because you just added another $7.42 per month to the deal.

We can't get greedy here. Going for $29 is going to make someone think twice and we might have a credibility problem and lose the deal. Go for a little bump just to give everyone that last bit of satisfaction before the deal is over. No one wants to feel like they've left something on the table. This last attempt is to either make the customer feel great about their negotiating wins or to squeeze just a little bit more out of it in gross—but either way, we want to shake their hand and wrap up the sale.

If we're still far apart on the deal by the time we reach the third pencil, we have to consider what we missed earlier on, whether it was in the first pencil or the first moments that we met them on the lot. In most situations, the third pencil should be the final one. Whoever presents it needs to be able to approve it on the spot or thank them for their time and walk them to the door. Usually, it's going to be the manager's responsibility, especially if it's a bigger bump.

When a deal is going down in flames—you're feeling too emotionally attached, you're feeling more like the customer's advocate—get a higher authority involved in the deal to try to close them before you burn them.

Goal: Finish the deal or walk the customer.

Remember: Everything that we did in the earlier steps of the sale will come back to help or haunt us here. If you're running into fourth and fifth pencils, it's time to evaluate everything that you're doing to see what's sending the negotiation off in the wrong direction.

Just like the closing tools, I have a lot here to get you started. When you're ready for more, head over to frictionlessnegotiating.com to level up your skills. No matter what, it's time to put the rubber to the road. Practice until you can't get it wrong!

CHAPTER 7

TOOLS FOR FRICTIONLESS NEGOTIATING

TIPS FOR A SUCCESSFUL NEGOTIATION

KEEP THE CUSTOMER BUSY WHEN THEY'RE ALONE

My dad always told me that an idle mind is the devil's workshop. Well, leaving the customer alone for too long can result in many negative outcomes. First of all, leaving the customer alone needs to be rare and, when it's necessary, you better keep it short. When this happens, you must have something to keep them busy. In the old days, it was a three-ring binder with a bunch of stuff in it, but in today's digital world it should be a tablet that you open to your dealership's social page where they can read reviews, watch walkaround videos, and see customer engagements. Bottom line: keep them busy and off their phone if at all possible.

DELIVERY AND CADENCE

Having confidence in what you say in the negotiation is critical, while having the proper delivery and cadence when you present the numbers can potentially make or break the deal. If the presentation is too slow or choppy, the customer will interrupt you and take control; if your cadence is too fast, your words will be ahead of their thoughts and the presentation will lose its effectiveness. Finding that sweet spot takes practice, but when you discover it, the initial presentation becomes seamless.

PRESENT TO DEFEND

Presenting the first pencil to a customer is more than just reading a bunch of numbers and hoping they pick one. A typical first pencil will consist of price, trade, down, and payment in some form—and if you're not skilled, it'll be four areas to lose gross or potentially the sale. It's about having confidence in your skills and focusing on the ultimate goal of completing the presentation of the pencil, then assuming the sale. Presenting to defend is making sure you don't overexplain every number on the worksheet. Otherwise, it'll result in a long, drawn-out grind. Keep your initial presentation short, sweet, and on point, with no nervous chatter that talks through the deal.

SHORT TERM AND CASH ARE KING

Anyone can sell a customer one car, but a true professional focuses on turning a one-time customer into a lifetime customer. Long-term success in the car business is about customer retention and managing their trade cycle. Unfortunately, too often we take the path of least resistance and jump right to presenting eighty-four months with zero down—which is bad for us, but it's horrible for the customer. They'll be lucky if they have equity in forty-eight months, and if they come back in two years to trade and find out how buried they are, they'll end up hating your guts. I'm not saying that the customer will sign off at forty-eight months with $6,700 down, but the more you get down with the shortest term possible, the better it will be, and this is best for all parties in the long run.

REFOCUS THE OBJECTION

Refocusing the customer's price or trade objections to down payment is critical for controlling and directing the negotiation. After your initial presentation of the first pencil, the customer may address the selling price or trade value, while we want to focus on down and payment to maximize gross and close on budget. The key to refocusing is to acknowledge their concern, followed by an either/or question based on the down payment. This allows you to determine whether it's a real objection or just a reflex response. Refocusing is typically effective once or twice, and if the customer redirects a third time, you have to negotiate on that objection.

FOCUS ON CUSTOMER BENEFITS

Everyone tunes in to their favorite radio station—WIIFM (*What's In It For Me*) and your customers are no different. Be prepared to justify your numbers and focus on selling the customer on their benefits. If their concern is down, then explain that the more they put down, the less they finance and the more they save in interest, not to mention they'll have more equity. If it's the payment and term, explain to them that it's based on an accelerated equity program and you may be able to extend the term. The bottom line is to always remember that the customer needs to have victories during the negotiation, so don't just *tell* them the benefits, *sell* them the benefits.

THE MAGIC PEN

We've all been told that we believe more of what we see than what we hear, and that couldn't be more true than during a negotiation. Being a great negotiator is more than just having a bunch of scripts and words. It's about mastering the art of using visuals with your scripts and words simultaneously. The positive impact on your negotiation can be as simple as crossing out your numbers and circling theirs to give them wins—or it can be as complex as developing the Total Cost of Ownership Close before their eyes. Whether it's just a small example or a detailed one, don't just tell it, *know* your purpose and develop the picture.

POWER OF SUGGESTION

Homer Simpson said, "There's no such thing as stupid questions, just stupid people that ask questions." Now, I'm not sure about that, but I do know that asking customers what they want to pay or what they're thinking is an easy way to get a ridiculous answer. Of course they'll lowball you—we would do the same thing if we were in their position. Instead of asking open-ended questions, always suggest a number to get their thinking up. Say things like "How close to $39,995 were you thinking? More like $39,500?" or "Were you thinking $6,700 down or maybe $5,000?" The goal of suggesting numbers is to control the conversation and pull out their top numbers so you can negotiate on the difference.

EASY BUMPS

Easy bumps are exactly what the title says they are—they help you get the customer to increase their price, payment, or down. The key to using easy bumps is timing, tone and inflection, and body language. When the customer gives you a number, it's important to respond immediately. For example, the customer says,

"We were thinking $425 per month."

Up to?

"Maybe $450."

For the car you really love?

"We can do $460, but that's the max."

To really get the most out of easy bumps, add body language like raising your hand in unison with your words. You'll find that the customer will typically give you one bump, and if you're good maybe two, but that's better than no bumps at all.

THE LAW OF DISAPPEARING DISCOUNTS

When negotiating a car deal, too often we tend to drop our numbers in large increments, and that makes it challenging to close the deal and extremely hard to hold gross. If you lower your price in $500 or $1,000 increments it makes the customer think big numbers also. Whether you're negotiating price, trade, or payment, always start with smaller numbers, then reduce the amount on each additional drop. For example, if your initial drop is $400 and the customer still won't go for it, the second drop should be $225, then the third $120, until there is no more room left. This principle is effective because subconsciously there is no more money left to give.

RECOMMIT EACH PENCIL

During a negotiation, a commitment isn't a one-time thing, it's an every time thing. You've presented to defend the numbers, justified and bumped the customer on down and payment, and now you need to be sure to corner and commit the customer. "Let me see if I have this right. Other than getting this for $2,250 down at $479 per month, is there any other reason we couldn't wrap this up?" If they say no, congratulations—you've just recommitted them. If they say yes, it's time to dig in and find out what's holding them back. Otherwise, you're just negotiating with yourself. Make sure to recommit the customer at the end of every pencil to ensure the negotiation is as frictionless as possible.

CLOSING ON YOUR NEGOTIATION

GAS SAVINGS CLOSE

The Gas Savings Close is a logical close that allows you to show the customer their future monthly fuel savings to help justify how they can afford their new payment. This comes in the second pencil, and the key is to know the math and write it out with them. (By the way, don't use if they're trading a Civic for a Suburban. Duh!)

MAINTENANCE CLOSE

The Maintenance Close leverages logic during the second pencil when you need to help the customer to justify stretching their budget. If the customer has spent $900 in repairs and maintenance over the last twelve months, it means they're spending $75 per month on average. That may be the money you need to close the deal and keep the gross intact.

TOTAL COST OF OWNERSHIP CLOSE

The Total Cost of Ownership Close is a combination of the customer's current payment and the Gas Savings, Maintenance, and potentially Insurance Savings Closes. This close is powerful because it logically breaks down the difference between the customer's actual current monthly expense versus what their total monthly payment will be on the new car. This close needs to be supported with a worksheet that shows a visual explanation.

COST PLUS CLOSE

The Cost Plus Close is for the customer that has done extensive research, is 100 percent price-focused, and thinks they should be able to buy the vehicle at or below invoice. This close is completely transparent, because the worksheet lists the MSRP and invoice, then subtracts the Factory Holdback to show the true dealer cost. It then adds fixed and semi-fixed expenses such as advertising cost per vehicle, average sales compensation, paperwork/DMV processing costs, and average vehicle holding/flooring expenses to determine the true cost to the dealership. Once true cost is determined, it adds in a fair profit, based on a predetermined percentage, and the negotiation is based on the percentage instead of the overall price.

REDUCE TO THE RIDICULOUS CLOSE

The Reduce to the Ridiculous Close utilizes a combination of mental involvement and logic to justify why the gap between us and the customer is insignificant and not worth missing out on the car they've worked hard for and deserve. When negotiating, it is best to focus on the smallest dollar amounts, because the biggest grosses can often be made when negotiating on the smallest numbers. The Reduce to the Ridiculous Close is most effective when the dollar amount is related to an everyday item, such as coffee or the pocket change they throw into a jar.

UNEVEN SPLIT CLOSE (OR THE ODDBALL SPLIT CLOSE)

The Uneven Split Close is a pattern interruption that is designed to get an even split. Asking a customer, "If we could split the difference, would you take it?" rarely results in an even split. Even the customer that may not be a skilled negotiator will usually split your split. The Uneven Split Close can be used in any situation you and the customer have a gap, such as $22,000 and $20,000. It's as simple as, "Other than getting my manager to split the difference and taking $21,750, is there any other reason we couldn't wrap this up?" The typical response is "That's not a fair split—a fair split is $21,000." At that point, you've at least got the customer thinking *up* to an even split, and that's the goal with this close.

REMOVABLE OBJECTION CLOSE

The Removable Objection Close works best when the customer wants more for their trade than it's worth and you need to get them to accept less to make the deal. To effectively use this close, there must be items on their vehicle that need reconditioning, and they need to be aware of them. This close allows you to give them a win because they get the number they want while allowing us a win at the same time. The key is to be positive, let them know you'll give them their number, and finish it up by giving them the choice of taking care of the needed reconditioning on their own or taking less and you'll take care of the repairs.

SERVICE CREDIT CLOSE

The Service Credit Close is a creative option to handle the customer that is still adamant about getting a discount during the second or third pencil. The customer gets the $500 or $1,000 discount/savings that they want in future dollars spent in your service department. The power of the close is that it gives the customer a win because they get 100 percent of the discount with only about 30 percent of the cost to the dealership. When those dollars are used in your service department, they will be billed at retail so that the dealership is still making a profit while retaining a customer.

PRE-PAID MAINTENANCE CLOSE

Like the Service Credit Close, the Pre-Paid Maintenance Close is another creative way to handle those times when the customer still wants a discount on the second or third pencil. This close will be dependent on the products and options that your dealerships offers. The term can be anywhere from twelve to thirty-six months, but the key is to show them the actual cash value so they see how it benefits them. This represents real dollars they will be saving and the benefit to you is that it can tie them to your dealership long-term, which will give you the opportunity to sell them future vehicles.

$100 BILL CLOSE

The $100 Bill Close is used during the negotiation when the customer's main focus is their trade. They tell you that they're going to hold off and sell it on their own because they want $8,500 for it and you're giving them $7,500. This close is a great way to handle that objection because it uses both mental involvement and logic. The reality is, what they want and what they'll actually get for it when they try to sell it on their own are two different things. The most effective way to start this close is with *Feel-Felt-Found* to lower their defenses—then walk them through a story of selling the car on their own, hitting the pain points they'll encounter, the customer grinding them, and the payments and maintenance they'll still be obligated to cover.

SHAKE AND BUMP CLOSE

The Shake and Bump Close is the final attempt to increase the gross and make sure you aren't leaving any money on the table. It is used on the last pencil when the manager has accepted their final offer and you know that you have a deal but you haven't told the customer yet. It's easy to focus on what you've already earned on the deal but this close will ensure that you don't miss out on that last bit of gross. The great thing about it is, it's a win/win for you either way and it'll make the customer feel that you are working for them. It's as simple as asking the customer, "My manager wanted me to ask you if you're going to let $7.42 a month keep you from getting your new car?" If they say "No"—you just say "Congratulations, that's exactly what I told him"—you just increased the gross. If they say "Yes"—you say "Congratulations, that's exactly what I told him"—you just found out that you got all you could, plus they'll know that you're looking out for them.

Either way, you and the customer both win, so have no fear, get out there and go for that last bump.

> ### ADDITIONAL TOOLS TO CLOSE THE DEAL
>
> - Use their next payment to increase the down payment and lower the payment.
> - Defer their first payment for sixty to ninety days.
> - Collect the sales tax to help reduce and close on the payment.
> - Show their insurance savings to justify their total monthly cost of ownership.
> - Use F&I cancelable for down payment.
>
> For more closing tools and resources, go to frictionless-negotiating.com.

CONCLUSION

Congratulations on making it all the way through this book. If you just turned to the last chapter first to get to the ending, flip back to page one and start over. We just covered a whole lot of information, and getting great at closing and negotiation needs that. It starts with obtaining as much knowledge as possible, turning that knowledge into skills, and using it to build your confidence.

Some of what we talked about went deep into situational techniques, while some of it was just about mindset. There's no way you can take all of it and run, and even if you did, I can't promise that it would make 100 percent of your sales win/win. What I can say is that there's no reason you can't learn and use it all to make your sales process frictionless.

Listen, I'm the guy who went to college for four years and

still couldn't manage an associate's degree. I started out washing cars. I promise you, anyone can learn how to be a great closer and negotiator. It's not easy, but what's your alternative? If you keep doing what you're doing, you'll keep getting what you're getting. And the only reason you're this far into the book is because you're tired of what you've been getting.

I always say it and I'll say it again: car sales will be the easiest high-paying job or the hardest low-paying job you'll ever have. The difference comes down to the choices that you make every day.

HARD-WON COMPETENCE

Most of us start out unconsciously incompetent, trying to make that low-paying job work. We want a good job, and car sales seems to be an answer, but we have no idea what good or bad looks like in that context. We simply don't know what we don't know. After a few difficult customer interactions, it becomes pretty clear that we're missing things—we're now consciously incompetent. This is where fight or flight kicks in. Our instincts say we should either fight against learning it or run away completely. It's not until we can embrace the lessons and practice the skills that we start to level up.

When everything changed during the recession and the

internet boom, as an industry we became consciously incompetent within the new world of car sales, and we went into fight-or-flight mode. We tried to keep doing business as usual, even though the customers were clearly showing us they needed something different.

I spent thirteen years off the sales floor, traveling around training people to do things the way that they've always been done. When I went back into sales after that, I realized many of the methods I was teaching were outdated and contradicted the process that was needed to handle the changes that had happened in the industry. The customer had changed too much, while we had stayed just the same.

Now, I only train techniques that are actively working, boots on the ground, face-to-face with customers and salespeople. Everything that I've outlined in this book came from those belly-to-belly interactions. We listened to customers, tried new techniques, and adapted until we could finally operate out of inspiration again, not desperation.

YOU MAKE IT
HAPPEN
WATCH IT
HAPPEN
OR FIND YOURSEL
SAYING
WHAT THE HELL JUS
HAPPENED

PERFECT PRACTICE MAKES PERFECT

You might or might not have support from your management staff as you practice these skills. Ideally, you'll be able to find another salesperson who shares your mindset and wants to learn and get better. Grab them, help each other, coach each other, and challenge each other. If you don't have someone like that around, that's fine too. Either way, it doesn't really matter. You can't leave your success up to someone else.

Take personal ownership. Learn and practice these skills. We can watch all the videos and read all the books on golf that we want, but our backswing won't get any better until we get out there and practice.

Read the scripts out loud over and over again until they're part of you and you can make them sound natural. Record yourself and watch for not only what you say but how you say it, what you look like, and how it comes across. Listen for a scripted sound, as well as whether it sounds natural or if the cadence is right. Know what your response should be in virtually every situation, and practice those responses until they're conversational.

Work on changing one step of your process at a time, and add things in as they become more natural. One thing will lead to the next, and before you know it you'll have your initial presentation script down pat. When you believe in that script and relay that in your body language and voice, it becomes less of a technique and more of a reflex. It's just genuinely what you *do*. Once you have that much down, the effect only grows from there.

Don't let the "what ifs" keep you from being great. Hone your skills, get better, and do everything you can to sell what you need to sell. It doesn't matter whether the dealership is having a bad month—do everything you can so that *you* don't have bad months anymore.

IF YOUR CUSTOMER'S FIRST—YOUR CAREER WILL LAST

When you get better at closing and negotiating, you're able to put your customers in better positions. When they walk away happy with their experience and in a loan or lease that they can handle, and when you follow up with them and keep that relationship going, they'll be that much more likely to come back to you for their trade cycle.

Long-term success in this industry cannot come from 100 percent fresh up traffic. We have to have repeat and referral customers. We have to manage trade cycles.

In the past, we've been heavily focused on immediate results. Follow-up calls take a back seat to activity on the lot. Contrary to common practices, however, what we can seal and deliver now doesn't actually matter as much as practicing process and procedure for what we can create long-term. We have to think bigger if we want to stick around.

Everything we do right now is actually a lagging indicator. You're not necessarily going to see results from it right now—the effects of our actions won't come back to us for thirty, sixty, ninety days. Yes, we need more traffic now. Yes, we need to sell cars and make money and feed the beast now. But we also have to fuel the future, or we'll become the next Kodak or Blockbuster or any other cultural staple that eventually became extinct.

Show me your average down payment or your average financing or lease term, and I'll show you what your future success in the car business will be. If your downs are low and your loans are extended on a regular basis, your future here is minimal. Our floor traffic is going down, not up. If you want to stick around, you have to build ongoing relationships based on trust and a solid trade cycle.

WHAT'S NEXT?

Jerry Seinfeld spent entire years creating one joke. Stephen Curry still practices shooting three-pointers every single day. Now that you have the understanding, tools, and techniques, it's time to put them into practice.

It's mundane. It's repetitive. It's boring. And you have to power through anyway.

Your career starts to build when you start having fun with it. To get to that point, you've got to challenge yourself. Turn your knowledge and skills into confidence, then turn the confidence into enthusiasm and transfer it to the customer. Get excited about the problems you're going to help them solve with the car they've been dreaming about owning. Look forward to finding that one who'll pay sticker or the other who will send their friends and family to you.

Dig deep until you find your competitive edge—the thing that makes you the Seinfeld or Curry of car sales. The thing that will bring people back to you over and over again so that your job becomes easy and your pay takes off. Then practice it over and over again until you can't get it wrong.

On our website, you'll find audio, video, and printable resources to help you. We also have online training, a shop filled with tools, and workshop schedules. Everything you might need to help you internalize the skills you recognize in this book can be found right there.

I'll tell you what I tell my classes at the end of our time together: successful people make a habit of doing what failures don't like to do.

Successful people are driven by the strength of their purpose. It propels them to their dreams and forces them to do all the things they don't want to do, so they can achieve the things they want to achieve.

It's easier to rationalize your disappointments than it is to realize your dreams. It's easier to be saturated with complacency than to be stirred up with passion. It's easier to be skeptical than successful. And when it comes right down to it, it's easier to belch out the baloney than it is to bring home the bacon. But doing what's easy will make a difficult J.O.B. (Just Over Broke), while doing the hard things will take your career to the next level.

IF YOU SAY YOU'RE GOING *TO START TOMORROW,* YOU'LL STILL BE *BROKE AND STRUGGLING* IN A YEAR

It'll be painful for a while, but there are two types of pain in life: good and bad. The good pain weighs ounces, while the bad pain weighs tons. The good pain is the *pain of discipline*. It's the discipline of doing the right thing because it's the right thing to do. Everything in this book, in my trainings, in this process takes effort. If you wait until you're motivated to do them, you'll never do them. Motivation is the byproduct of action and the best thing about the pain of discipline is that the pain only lasts until you do it—and that's where the bad pain comes in.

The pain that weighs tons is loaded down with regret. I wish I did my follow-up. I wish I'd worked on negotiating for bigger downs. I wish I'd worked on negotiating for shorter term. I wish I'd set goals. I wish I'd practiced my closes.

All of those *coulda-woulda-shouldas* are wrapped up in what we didn't do, the *pain of regret*, and that kind of pain sticks around forever. Don't get buried under that weight. Get out of your comfort zone and start practicing now, so that later you can get more out of life than you ever thought you could.

This career can be everything you thought it would be— the question is whether you're going to step up to the challenge. If you're ready, it's time to get to work. I've got your back.

ABOUT THE AUTHOR

TIM KINTZ is the president of The Kintz Group, the automotive industry's premier sales and management training company. Tim started The Kintz Group after reentering the retail side of the business as a general manager and seeing the need for up-to-date training. A graduate of the NADA Academy, Tim has worked in just about every position in the dealership and can still be found on the showroom floor, working deals alongside salespeople and managers. Tim has delivered hands-on coaching, workshops, and presentations in large cities and rural communities alike. His strategies are relevant and proven to work everywhere cars are sold.